"Aric, Doug, and Nick are ridiculous, but *Never Pray Again* is exactly the kind of tomfoolery the church needs. Too many Christians speak holy sounding words, and assume their work for the good of creation is done. *Never Pray Again* offers us practical action words, and gets us to a place where we understand the truth spoken by Teresa of Avila: that 'Christ has no hands and feet now but ours.'"

— Landon Whitsitt, author of *Open Source Church*

"Never pray again? The very thought feels like a slap in the face of our faith! But through their engaging and provocative words, Aric Clark, Doug Hagler, and Nick Larson teach us how to attach legs to our laments, give teeth to our supplications, and put skin on our spiritual lives. Read *Never Pray Again*. But more importantly, practice it. For if we all engaged in such Christianity, our world would be transformed."

— Carol Howard Merritt, author of *Tribal Church*

"Filled with questions and doubts, many Christians have given up on prayer. Enter Aric Clark, Doug Hagler, and Nick Larson's urgent manifesto *Never Pray Again*. Witty, provocative, insightful, and practical. Here is a bracing and bold vision of prayer with the potential to radically transform our lives and faith communities. Read, go, and do."

— Richard Beck, associate professor of psychology, Abilene Christian University

D1316846

"No longer does 1 + 1 have to equal 2. No longer do we have to act as extras in the 'Walking Dead.' Liberation from formulaic certainty is a freeing and life-giving. Yet liberation from formulaic certainty can also be a genuinely scary place. *Never Pray Again* is simply not just a book about prayer—it is a manifesto of liberation, illuminating outside-of-the-box avenues in which we as the creation can communicate with The Creator. Writers Aric, Doug, and Nick, in the voice of the pastor and the prophet, give us the permission to live into the resurrection. And yes, some of us do need the permission to live into the resurrection—shattering our paradigms of stagnancy, breathing new vitality into our everyday rhythms of living."

—Phil Shepherd, aka The Whiskey Preacher, cofounder of Eucatastrophe missional community in Fort Worth, Texas

"At first glance it may seem counterintuitive to invite Christians to never pray again, but Aric, Doug, and Nick have something up their sleeves that deserves a hearing. By drawing on their trademark wit, wisdom, and sensibility, they poignantly describe how Christians can better appropriate gifts of the Christian tradition, such as prayer, in order to recapture the best of what these practices harbor, which is nothing less than the mending and repairing of the world and all who live in it. This book is a must read for all Christians longing for prayer to be understood less as an individualistic exchange with a supernatural being on high and more as a call to respond to the very real needs of the world God longs to liberate."

—Phil Snider, senior minister, Brentwood Christian Church, Springfield, Missouri, and editor of *The Hyphenateds*

NEVER PRAY AGAIN

LIFT YOUR HEAD, UNFOLD YOUR HANDS, AND GET TO WORK

ARIC CLARK,
DOUG HAGLER,
AND NICK LARSON

CHALICE®
PRESS

ST. LOUIS, MISSOUR

www.chalicepress.com

Print: 9780827225251   EPUB: 9780827225268   EPDF: 9780827225275

**Library of Congress Cataloging in Publication Data
available upon request.**

Printed in the United States of America.

To Julia, Pam, and Stacia for making us better and making this possible.

Thank you to those people who have supported us, challenged us, and gone ahead of us. It would be foolish to think we did anything alone.

Contents

Introduction

"I prayed for twenty years but received no answer until I prayed with my legs."—Frederick Douglass

Imagine never praying again.

Ask anyone—prayer is the cornerstone of the Christian life. Prayer is the most popular activity in every church, rivaled only by potlucks. Prayer is proffered by well-meaning churchgoers as the solution to every problem, and prayer is what you most often get when you ask a church for help. There are countless books, pamphlets, videos, conferences, retreat centers, experts, and devotional guides that will teach you how to pray.

Not this book.

This book tries to teach another way. We want you to lift your head, open your eyes, unfold your hands, and get to work. It's our observation that prayer is often a substitute for action. So if we want you to act instead of praying, what would we suggest? This book is our answer. We hope that after you read this book you will never pray again.

Perhaps the very idea of not praying sends you to the edge of a panic attack. If so, then we gently recommend you put this book down. A huge array of other books will be better suited to your spiritual needs. If you decide to join us on this adventure, we will deconstruct the most ancient and beloved Christian tradition, and hopefully put better things in its place. We welcome you to join us.

Perhaps the idea of never praying again causes you to feel a wave of relief. If so, this might be just the book you are looking for, but you too might find things you treasure being reinterpreted in surprising ways. We hope you enjoy the ride.

Perhaps you are already someone who does not pray. If so, that is an excellent beginning, but removing the obstacle is only the start. The road stretches ahead of you, and you will find things in this book to help you continue on your journey.

If you're still reading, then you must be at least willing to entertain the possibility of giving up prayer. In fact, you won't even see the word prayer again in this book until the closing chapter. That's because we never want you to pray again. Instead of praying, do these things, and live...

Awaken!

Whenever Mark needs to rest in God's presence, he simply has to be still, close his eyes, and fold his hands. It helps if he can be in a quiet, peaceful place. This is what he was always taught to do, and it is all he knows to do. Every day, Mark takes this time to be with God in private. He is still, closes his eyes, folds his hands, and his conscience goes to sleep.

Shambling Faithful Hordes

For many people, Christian discipleship is sleepwalking. We inhabit a world of dreams and imagination, of theology and interpretation, of jargon and tradition. Worship services follow the same pattern week after week, and we can just coast through. Christian leaders can, and do, phone it in. We stand, we sit, some of us kneel, we turn to face the cross, we bow our heads, we take a morsel of bread and a sip from a cup, and we proclaim our work done. Our practices focus us on our inner world: our relationship with God, our conscience, our beliefs and thoughts, whether we are "saved." We spend lots of time with eyes closed, both literally and figuratively.

This is Zombie Christianity.

The original idea of the zombie comes from a supposed practice in Haitian Vodoun wherein a person is drugged and brought near death, so close that they believe that they died. They are then resuscitated and kept in a mesmerized, semi-conscious state through the use of drugs and neurotoxins from animals such as the puffer fish. They shamble around, lost in a daze, and are highly suggestible. They forget themselves, and spend whatever life is left for them in the service of the *houngan* or *mambo*. This image has more to do with science fiction than fact, but it has since grown from that original idea to inspire a whole subculture of zombie books, zombie films, zombie TV shows and zombie fans. There are zombie walks at conventions and zombie runs for charity. The shambling Vodoun slave has been replaced, for the most part, with the flesh-eating hordes. The core image remains consistent, however: a person who has lost personhood and is now mindlessly driven by base desires, whether as a slave to black magic or infected by a virus that causes them to hunger for flesh.

In Christianity we talk about dying with Christ, but most of the time it is more like a zombie-death. We come close to death, but don't go all the way, and then we are filled with toxic ideas and practices that numb our senses to the world around us. It results in a church that has no sense of itself. We take our leave from our supposedly modern, information-age society and return to a world of superstition, misogyny, racism, class differences, and constant infighting over issues such as marriage, homosexuality, or what we imagine the end of the world will look like (and who will be invited). Neither truly alive nor truly dead, we are mindlessly driven by base concerns for social standing, security, comfort, and reassurance.

We shamble through life, focused on our supposed relationship with Jesus, and the rightness of our beliefs, and the relationships we have with people who are just like us; all the while the world around us continues in its conflagration of violence, oppression, and injustice. This is sleepwalking: numbly shambling through life, from one habit to the next, never truly alive and aware. Despite Jesus telling us whatever we fail to do for others we fail to do for him, and Amos calling on us to let justice roll down like waters,[1] we are asleep on the job.

Jesus tells the story of a wealthy landowner who has a fantastic harvest, so good that all of the surplus grain won't fit in his barn. It never occurs to him to share that surplus with other people. It isn't maliciousness, he just goes about making his decisions the same way we would, trying to ensure his own future and enjoy the fruits of his labor. So he tears the barn down and builds much bigger storehouses to hold all the grain. When he's done he goes to sleep thinking he is secure for years to come, but Jesus ends the story by shouting, "You fool! Tonight your life is demanded of you!"[2] Having been numbed

---

1. Matthew 25:31–41; Amos 5:21–24.
2. Author paraphrase of Luke 12:13–21

by a life lived out of communion with people in need, the wealthy landowner is surprised by death and his harvest is wasted.

In a zombie-apocalypse story, such as *The Walking Dead* or *28 Days Later*, we see people in the aftermath of the collapse of society. We can easily imagine the rotting grain storehouses of the wealthy landowner in and amongst the abandoned supermarkets and shattered storefront windows. No one knew that their lives would be demanded of them, and we are left with a stark image of the emptiness of a life spent storing things up.

This same emptiness applies to much of the Christian life: the emptiness of being right about the nuances of theology; the emptiness of preaching good news to the poor while wearing a five-thousand-dollar suit; the emptiness of interminable altar calls that never change lives in the long-term; the emptiness of arguing about the Creation Museum[3] or the Jesus Seminar.[4] There is a great deal of toxicity throughout Christian practice, and through slow accumulation we are poisoned, our senses and wits dulled, until we too are shambling through the ruins of what might have been.

Our comfort has lulled us to sleep, promising a restful night and pleasant dreams. We're oblivious to the stakes of our complacency. Like the wealthy landowner, one day our lives will really be demanded of us. We won't be undead, we'll just be dead. When it comes, will we suddenly realize we've been sleepwalking through most of our lives? Or have we become so thoroughly anesthetized that we think a life spent sleepwalking is all there is?

Buying a Cornetto

ARIC

The best zombie movie ever made is Shaun of the Dead. *Don't disagree with me. I will fight you on this.*

In the opening minutes of the film we are treated to a variety of sequences in which the protagonist, Shaun, is surrounded by bleary-eyed, shambling, mindless, ordinary people at work, on the bus, and sitting in a pub. A cell phone rings and five people simultaneously reach into their pockets and look at their phones with

---

3. The Creation Museum in Petersburg, Kentucky, is an institute created to maintain popular support for creationism. It has exhibits such as Adam & Eve in the Garden of Eden alongside dinosaurs.

4. The Jesus Seminar was a group of scholars founded in the 1980s that studied scripture critically, trying to propose a new perspective on the historical person of Jesus of Nazareth and the development of the early Christian tradition.

blank stares. Conversations are had in which neither party really hears the other over their distraction, and the dialogue is just a series of non sequiturs punctuated by rhetorical "whats?"

As Shaun sleeps through his job and his relationships, he is oblivious to the increasing panic in the background. Strangers are seen running from unknown danger. An ambulance screeches to a halt behind Shaun and first responders tend to a man who has just died at the steering wheel of his car. Leaving his favorite pub, "The Winchester," Shaun thinks the couple against the wall in the alley is making out, but while Shaun isn't watching the woman bites the man's shoulder and his head flops back at an impossible angle.

The peak of both humor and tension in this first act is when Shaun awakens with a hangover and goes to the local store to buy a Cornetto (an ice cream cone dipped in chocolate). The moment he steps out his door it is clear the Zombie Apocalypse has arrived. Car windows are smashed, a distant alarm is ringing, mangled corpses lay around corners and crumpled on front steps. Shaun sees none of this. He goes into the store and opens a fridge without seeing the bloody handprints on the glass. He slips in something without looking down to learn what. He walks back to his house, passing a dozen lethargic undead—only one of whom he notices and mistakes for a panhandling vagrant. At any moment, you expect him to get attacked, and yet he makes it all the way back into his house without ever realizing he has just taken a stroll through a zombie-infested wasteland.

It turns out the real zombie is Shaun himself, and the tragi-comic arc of the film's narrative shows him waking up to the decrepit state of all his relationships just as circumstances may cause him to lose everything.

A Terrible Idea

Fortunately, there is no reason we need to remain asleep. Zombie-hood is not a permanent condition. There is a cure for the toxic ideas and practices that put us to sleep. We have to get over some of the false ideas we have about God and about ourselves. We have to recover from the idea that following Jesus is primarily about our inner life. We have to wake up.

That being said, waking up is a terrible idea. The more aware you become, the more difficult it is to remain the same. Your perceptions will change; your relationships will change; your politics will change. It will become much harder to wait for God to do everything for you, and it will become very painful to just accept things as they are. What was a comfortable life becomes not only uncomfortable but untenable.

The world of violence, exploitation, injustice, oppression, and bigotry depends on the unthinking support of zombie hordes. It is absolutely crucial to the "powers that be" that we remain "believers" rather than "doers," that we never truly come alive, and that we continue to choose to be ignorant of what is going on around us. Everything will stay as it is so long as we continue to meet in our safe buildings, segregating ourselves from "them" all in the name of false belonging. Making excuses is a lot easier than making peace. Believing in Jesus as our "personal" Lord and Savior is far easier than the Ministry of Reconciliation. Working on our own moral shortcomings is a cake-walk compared to walking out into the world that crucified Christ and seeking to follow Christ regardless.

If you want peace and prosperity and the acceptance and respect of your peers, if you want safety and security and social status, if you want certainty and comfort and confidence, remain asleep.[5]

A Robot Army

Being awake means being aware. It means having your attention properly trained on the world around you, which is very easy to say you'll do—and nearly impossible to maintain. Awareness requires constant vigilance alloyed with a gentleness of spirit that allows you to forgive your inevitable lapses and simply return your focus where it belongs. Your greatest ally in the hard work of cultivating awareness is empathy.

Empathy is the capacity to recognize and relate to the emotions of other people. What empathy does is shock us out of our self-absorption. When someone near us experiences pain and we see and respond to that pain, we are honing our awareness, as well as honoring the value and dignity of that person. We are shaken awake emotionally, as we would if we were experiencing the pain ourselves.[6]

Without empathy we are robots. Robots cannot have empathy. Even very advanced robotic faces that try to mimic empathy just end

---

5. Seriously. Put the book down. No one will ever know.
6. For more on how empathy functions in the brain, from Psychology Today: http://www.psychologytoday.com/blog/fulfillment-any-age/201103/when-disaster-strikes-others-how-your-brain-responds

up looking creepy, and the best that a machine can do is to pass a Turing Test—to come off as *appearing* human. Unlike robots, human beings are built for empathy. Whole systems in the brain, the systems that we share with all other mammals, are there just to connect with other people emotionally.

Our stories come alive as we come to understand *other* people's stories. Part of the value of things such as film or fiction, games or theater, is that we get to vicariously experience life through someone else. The best actors and artists can make us empathize with imaginary people; they are drawing on our natural inclination to empathize that is part of what it means to be human. Through stories, we are able to live many lives, at least in part, but this involvement can be painful when we encounter the pain in those lives.

What we understand to be true is impacted by what those around us understand. Feelings such as joy, anger, or fear are literally contagious, and unconsciously pass from one person to another.[7] The idea that we are autonomous individuals has been rendered ridiculous by our study of the mind and brain. Empathy is a particular ability that can and should be strengthened and cultivated, but in doing this we are building upon a capacity that is basic to almost all of us. We are made to connect, and that explains, in part, how much effort it requires to dull that very ability.

Ironically, one of the greatest inhibitors of empathy, dulling our sense of other people, may be religion. All our hand clasping, head bowing, and pious mumbling may be working directly against the goal of waking up by subtly programming us to act out of obligation rather than compassion. Researchers at the University of California at Berkeley and San Francisco found in three separate studies that the less religious a person was, the more likely he or she was to be motivated by compassion to help others.[8] The more religious a person was, the more likely it was that he or she reported feeling little or no compassion toward the suffering of others, even if the person still felt obligated to help. How can this be?

Psychologists have begun to call this the Macbeth Effect, after the character Lady Macbeth in Shakespeare's famous Scottish play.

---

7. For more on emotional contagion, from Wikipedia: http://en.wikipedia.org/wiki/Emotional_contagion

8. http://spp.sagepub.com/content/4/1/31.abstract, "My Brother's Keeper: Compassion Predicts Generosity More Among Less Religious Individuals" Journal of Social Psychological and Personality Science (July 2012).

During a pivotal scene in that play, after Lady Macbeth has committed a bloody murder to protect her husband, she is haunted by the feeling of having blood on her hands, which she cannot wash off no matter how hard she tries. The connection between her conscience and the physical act of washing her hands turns out to be a profound insight. Not only can a guilty conscience make us feel physically unclean, but if we engage in a physical cleansing process our conscience quiets back down. This works with guilt as well as a variety of other emotions. When we engage in a ritual connected with the emotion in question it dulls the edge and softens the urgency of the emotional impulse.

The Christian life offers an array of rituals perfect for deadening your capacity for empathy and turning us into robots that act out of obligation, but not out of compassion. In worship we praise the transcendent and eternal, making what is finite and immediate seem paltry by comparison. We confess our sins silently, or in private, or through vague wording, which keeps the truth of our lives from ever having to be expressed directly to other human beings. We spiritualize our struggles rather than directly confronting and expelling the poison in our behavior. We put our hope in supernatural healing rather than seeking concrete and attainable wholeness. We call on God to intercede and let people around us go on suffering. We hide our needs from each other at church while piously repeating slogans about God's providential care. Confronted with unavoidable pain, we seek refuge in trite answers rather than grieving with honesty. We offer token thanks in our liturgy, but live ungrateful lives. We sing love songs all Sunday long, but go right back to hating our enemies Monday morning.

These rituals can program us to be unresponsive. They tick off the to-do-list boxes, which gives us the feeling of having practiced compassion without actually having to practice it. This is part of what Marx meant when he called religion the "opium of the people,"[9] or what Freud meant by calling religion an illusion concocted to meet

---

9. It is worth reading the quote from Karl Marx in its full context. From the never-published A Contribution to the Critique of Hegel's Philosophy of the Right: "Religious suffering is, at one and the same time, the expression of real suffering and a protest against real suffering. Religion is the sigh of the oppressed creature, the heart of a heartless world, and the soul of soulless conditions. It is the opium of the people. The abolition of religion as the illusory happiness of the people is the demand for their real happiness. To call on them to give up their illusions about their condition is to call on them to give up a condition that requires illusions. The criticism of religion is, therefore, in embryo, the criticism of that vale of tears of which religion is the halo."

deep psychological needs.[10] Religion practiced this way is worse than just a crutch to help us get through the week; it is programming that turns us into robots, only capable of being obedient citizens, voracious consumers, and docile workers. Robots ready to serve in the robot army. Robots who are slaves to our programming, whether that programming is partisan politics or religious sectarianism. Separated from each other and numbed to each other's experiences, we can become inhumane, even inhuman.

Spawn of My Father the Devil

DOUG

I was recently banned from a LinkedIn group for Christian pastors and leaders, and it happened like this: the group is aimed at discussion, and we got onto the topic of creationism versus evolution. I quickly realized that I was the only person involved in the conversation who was not an ardent young-Earth creationist. I'm normally a person who enjoys a good discussion or debate—I find them to be fun, sometimes I learn something, and I learn to express myself a little bit better each time. So I dove in. I said something I felt was innocuous, to the effect of, "I think it's important to take science seriously, and to look at people who don't have an agenda and what they say about the natural world. I don't see a reason to be afraid of reason," something like that.

Next came a barrage of comments that were, in retrospect, kind of hilarious. One pastor declared that I was the spawn of my father, the Devil, clearly committed to destroying everyone's faith (I assure you he is the well-paid leader of a huge Christian community—scary in itself). Another Christian leader scoffed that I would be so easily taken in by the worldwide conspiracy of Godless scientists who teach the religion of evolution. A half-dozen or so quoted scripture at me, sometimes in ALL CAPS. A few other Christian leaders lectured me on the foolishness of evolution from a rational perspective—a couple of them had degrees in biblical studies or theology, which of course made them experts on biology and genetics.

Being called the spawn of the Devil for something I felt was innocuous was off-putting, and by the end of the day I found I was no longer a group member and was barred from posting again. I had run up against

---

10. We highly recommend Richard Beck, The Authenticity of Faith: The Varieties and Illusions of Religious Experience (Abilene: Abilene Christian University Press, 2012) for a deep exploration of Sigmund Freud's criticism of religion from a Christian perspective.

a great deal of programming all at once. These poor people were on such feeble footing that they were terrified of ideas. They already had the answers, thank-you-very-much, and anyone who had any questions or (God forbid!) differing answers was devil-spawn. The programming was so deep, the fear so rooted, that they couldn't even be polite about booting me.

Enslaved to Our Programming

The particular type of programming Christians are most susceptible to is dogma. Dogmatism takes a thinking, feeling person and replaces him or her with a simple algorithm—predictable results every time. When the articles of faith become non-negotiable, which by definition dogmas are, then we are reduced to the function of replicating ideas like theological copy-machines. Religion becomes a game of who can accumulate the most replicators—who can have the most people agreeing to a given set of dogmas.

The results of this mindless replication range from sad to ridiculous to downright harmful. It is sad when people are deprived of the freedom to think for themselves, form their own opinions, and take into account their own experiences. It is ridiculous when the need to replicate in order to fit in with a religious community leads someone to buy into young-Earth creationism or the magic of positive thinking. It is harmful when this replication means that large segments of society are comfortable referring to women who use contraceptives as prostitutes, or denying rights to a certain group or class of people, or resorting to violence in order to achieve their ends.

Dogmatism is widespread. It does not only issue from the Congregation for the Doctrine of the Faith[11] and the Answers in Genesis[12] crowd. It arises in subtle forms within every group of likeminded people. It preys upon our desire to conform and it offers a compelling defense for itself: it masquerades as Truth. It is a program that whispers to us, "Don't you want to hold to the Truth? Why would you entertain lies and half-truths if you could be one of the few who know the Truth?" Dogmatism takes what is natural, our need to belong, and turns it against us by making us insecure and defensive. It takes what is commendable, a thirst for truth, and turns it into

---

11. The Congregation for the Doctrine of the Faith is the oldest of the nine congregations of the Roman Curia. It is the body responsible for overseeing official Roman Catholic doctrine.

12. Answers in Genesis is an apologetics ministry behind the Creation Museum and a lot of pamphlets and curriculum supporting creationism.

an inquisition that tolerates no doubts and denies any evidence that contradicts its assertions.

Because of its role in building group cohesion, waking up from dogmatism often entails a period of rebellion. When we reject ideas and habits that previously defined us, it can be a painful break. Waking up may result in the end of friendships, a rise in anxiety, and a sense that much of value is being lost. Insecurity and frustration can lead us to be less than gracious toward our former robot peers. No one is more obnoxious than the recent convert, from the newly-minted vegan to the refugee fleeing Evangelicalism. Most likely our period of waking up will leave us with a lot to apologize for later. It is common and natural to over-correct in this way, to overreach once our hands are no longer tied.

The temptation of the former robot is to try to slap your friends and family out of it, but our job is to awaken ourselves, not our neighbors. How many of us came home from our freshman year of college with new books under our arms determined to enlighten our parents? Not only is this kind of idea-slapping impolite, it is spectacularly ineffective. Awakening is not something you can do for someone else. Nor is it a one-time event that, having been through it, you can just sit back and watch the people behind you on the road floundering, self-satisfied. If you commit to waking up, you will find yourself shuddering to alertness again and again through layers of programming nested like Russian dolls in your mind.

The people around us do have a role to play in our quest to wake up from being made into robots: they are opportunities for us to practice empathy. More than merely being aware of people around us, we have to recognize that they are people and not things—that they have intrinsic value, and dignity, and the right to decide for themselves. Rather than seeking to manipulate other people for our own ends, we come to them with humility, openness, and curiosity. Instead of working to make strange people more like us, we honor their strangeness, realize that we surely seem strange to them, and seek to understand rather than control them. In practicing empathy, we seek to see inside other people, to stand where they stand in our imaginations, and to consider their needs as equivalent to our own.

Empathy will make you a less efficient, less effective robot. You will slow down, and may no longer produce and consume the most products possible. You will change in response to the people around you, and will no longer be an effective idea-replicator, because new ideas will be arising all the time. You will be unable to participate in society without at least a little pain, because you will empathize with all the people around you who are being treated like machines. Yet, in order to be awake, we must practice empathy. We must see other people as not just a means to an end, but as infinitely worthwhile, infinitely interesting, in their own right and on their own terms. In practicing empathy, we can reject our programming and become human again.

Domesticated

Those of us who are in the church are accustomed to being called sheep. Christ is known as the Good Shepherd. We refer to a pastor's "flock," and even the term "pastor" that we commonly use for Protestant clergy comes from a word to describe someone who takes care of domesticated animals.

This is a pretty offensive metaphor if you think about sheep for even a moment. Sheep run away from anything that is frightening. They remain in flocks and, once a few start running, the rest will follow, even if they don't understand what is going on. Lost sheep are helpless—they are food for wolves unless a shepherd comes to find them and leads them back to the flock. The purpose of a sheep is to eat—to wander around, mindlessly consume, and to produce things for others. A sheep is there to make wool, and milk, and ultimately meat. When a sheep dies, it just dies. To a human eye, sheep are indistinguishable from each other. There are no brilliant sheep or creative sheep or sinister sheep.

Now, imagine a Christian who is not awake. It is easy to observe Christians running away even from harmless entertainment: rock 'n' roll, Dungeons & Dragons, or Harry Potter. There is nothing actually threatening about these things, but they startle the sheep and so the flock responds unthinkingly. Christians have a flock mentality— it is important to join, to attend, to show up, but that's about it. Go along with what is happening around you, and you'll be just fine. If a Christian becomes lost—doubting or questioning what is widely accepted, the response is not to take the doubts and questions seriously—the task of church leadership is to lead them back to the fold. There is no sense that a "lost" sheep might have discovered something better than what everyone is accustomed to. Christians are often taught to be indistinguishable—to believe the same things and engage in the same few practices and show up on the same day to the same events. As long as they are filling the collection plate, the church is assumed to be doing well—resurfacing their parking lot and adding a new building, or installing a sound board and digital projector. These are all signs of supposed health.

Of course, sheep require a shepherd. Due to the domestication process, sheep can no longer survive on their own. They are optimized for what we want from them and unable to defend themselves or respond to challenges. We have made them that way over a long period of time. In a way, the sheep do flourish—they are born and live and die, they don't have to worry about predators most of the time, and they are led to the greenest pastures. In a similar way, many Christians are insulated by Christian subculture, so that they only have to listen to Christian music and read Christian books and go to Christian events—and not even broadly Christian, but—in the U.S. at least—very specifically conservative Evangelical Christian. These Christians are also led to the green pastures—megachurches and bestselling "spiritual" books and charming pastors—and, in a very limited way, perhaps, they flourish in this domestication. Over generations, whole communities can forget that they were ever free and wild.

It takes effort to forget that God is wild, but we are quite capable of it. We have stories of God's wild wakefulness: speaking in fire and whirlwinds, driving people out into the wilderness, scattering the proud, overturning tables and nations; the God of behemoth and leviathan, of thunder and hail, of feast and famine; of dreams and wonders. To sheep, these are all terrifying things, threatening to their comfort and security. To the wakeful, this is merely life, and what it means to be alive.

Hipster Flocks

NICK

Have you ever been to an Emergent church event? Do you check out those conferences that feature the biggest and the brightest alternative to sheeplike churchianity? Then like me you've probably noticed that most of us tend to look the same. We tend to be slightly stylish, younger, predominantly male white dudes with thick horned-rimmed glasses, MacBook laptops, and most likely designer shoes.

Now I say this in the most loving way possible, typing on my MacBook laptop, but seriously... We are just another subculture falling victim to the same patterns of mindless conformity, while we talk revolution and sip lattes. It seems to me that my own particular form of flock mentality comes down to wearing a button down and skinny jeans, and sporting a tattoo or two.

I've been to way too many conferences that start out talking about the future of church and end up only complaining about the last form of church. It seems like every time we feel compelled to walk a different path, we end up just falling into another herd.

This is why awakening is an ongoing process, not a one-time conversion. Even when you've stripped away a layer of flock mentality, others are lurking beneath. Perhaps this is why Jesus said that his followers have no place to rest their heads: following Christ in this way may result in you being cut off from the flock. There will be other pilgrims on the road with you, but they will all look and sound different than you. There might not be a pair of skinny jeans among them.

The One Who Is Awake

The domesticated sheep are those who have been changed over time to become passive, but we are invited by Jesus himself to do greater things than he did.[13] We have been lulled into a specifically Christian form of passivism, bending our knees and folding our hands and waiting for Someone Else to do what needs to be done. The slumber of Church has not only kept us from being of use to others, it has kept us from being truly awake to God. If we are shambling around like zombies, if we are going through the motions like machines, if we are bleating in unison as sheep, we cannot be with God.

God is the one who is awake—God neither slumbers nor sleeps. God in Christ did not sleep, but was aware of what was going on around him at all times. Jesus was able to change his plans and even reinterpret ancient traditions in response to what he perceived. Is it lawful to work on the Sabbath? Maybe, if your child falls down a well or if your animal is stuck in a ditch or if the hungry need to be fed. For Jesus, there was no doctrine that was more powerful than the context of genuine human need. In a sense, this is a "doctrine" of wakefulness

---

13. John 14:12.

and responsiveness, rather than a rigid code requiring blinders and an anesthetized conscience.

Not only does God perceive; God responds. God is moved with pity and joy, regret and wrath. God hears Ishmael in the wilderness and responds to him, taking care of him and his mother Hagar when even Abraham and Sarah had cast them out to die.[14] God is not a machine and is never predictable—God is able to have a change of heart or mind in response to what human beings do. Abraham negotiates with God, and God is willing to change the plans for Sodom and Gomorrah.[15] Moses intercedes for the people of Israel and God chooses not to destroy the Hebrews who are worshiping the golden calf.[16] God is moved by the change of heart in Nineveh, showing mercy on a people marked for destruction. Jonah, still shambling, bleating, and enslaved by dogmatic programming, can do nothing but climb a hill outside the city to sulk.[17]

Again and again we find stories about God in which God changes and the people do not. God makes justice and equality a priority when people were still focusing on performing the right ceremonies. God shows mercy when the people only want, or expect, vengeance. God demonstrates wrath even on religious leaders who are still expecting that God is on their side. This is because God is awake and alive when we are so often asleep and dead inside. Howard Thurman said, "Don't ask what the world needs. Ask what makes you come alive, and go do it. Because what the world needs is people who have come alive."[18]

Our first, some might say only, job is to be awake as God is awake, responsive as God is responsive; concerned with justice when those around us are going through the motions of piety; showing mercy when we might have a right to revenge; challenging the powerful when we are supposed to just go along and fit in and keep quiet. This is the Christian life, a life lived awake and mindful, connected to other people and to the world around us. It is a life—lively, free, and wild.

***

---

14. Genesis 16.

15. Genesis 18:16–33. Although God changed the plan from "destroy Sodom and Gomorrah immediately" to "preserve Sodom and Gomorrah if Abraham can find a few righteous souls", it sadly still resulted in the destruction of the cities.

16. Exodus 32:7–14.

17. Jonah 3—4.

18. Gil Bailie's *Violence Unveiled*, p. xv

Whenever Amber thinks about the prom, she gets angry. Her friend Chloe has been dating her girlfriend Naomi for six months, and they posted to Facebook about going to prom together, Chloe in a tux and Naomi in a beautiful matching gown. Word got out, and, suddenly, with the support of the PTA and local churches, the principal was declaring that they were banned from prom. At church that Sunday, Amber's pastor preached about the importance of "traditional marriage," and it was clear about whom he was talking. So Amber is angry, and she has a plan. Together with a few dozen other students and some of their parents, she'll be throwing a party at the local VFA banquet hall. Everyone will be invited. It'll be on prom night, and her friends Chloe and Naomi will be there.

Experiments in Awakening

■ Listen deeply to someone who is wrong (and do not correct that person). Fight every urge to open your mouth, and instead set aside your own opinions and try to understand what this person is trying to tell you.

■ List your actual beliefs and compare them to the official beliefs of your sect, or, if you aren't part of any sect, compare them to the beliefs of your peers. Look at what is consistent and what isn't. Are you just parroting dogma, or is this what you really believe? Do you want to change how you live, or do you want to change what you say you believe?

■ Skip church (or another regular religious or spiritual practice) and volunteer instead. Compare the experiences, and decide which one you want to attend next time.

Praise!

Molly raises her hands high and sings God's praises at the top of her lungs. The beauty of her Lord Jesus flows through her, and she revels in the wonder of His precious love. As the congregation recites a psalm she joins in, offering her thoughts of joy and gratitude to God her Father, for all the wonderful things He created, and the way that He loves her even though she is a sinner. She wants to praise her savior all the day long, just like the hymn she used to sing as a kid, but suddenly a man climbs into the pew next to her reeking of urine and alcohol. She wrinkles her nose, politely so he cannot see, and moves to a new spot before he can ask her for money.

Ugliness Unredeemed

Everyone praises what they think is praiseworthy. Calling something beautiful when it is in fact widely regarded as beautiful seems at best to be redundant. No one is going to be shocked by who is named Sexiest Woman or Sexiest Man Alive in a given year, or what the Prom King and Queen look like.[1] No one is going to refuse to coo at your child or say, "What an ugly baby! But I bet she has character."

Praising beauty is as worthless as praising winners. Winners are the people we praise by default—we don't give gold medals to 27th place, and we don't give scholarships for Honorable Mention. Everyone knows a trophy for Most Improved Player means nothing.

---

1. Every now and then we're pleased to be proven wrong. There have been a few cases of high schools, such as the one in Sanford, Massachusetts, electing surprising Prom Kings and Queens. In 2011 Sanford elected a young gay couple Christian Nelsen and Caleb Jett Prom Queen and King, respectively.

The successful, the winners, are the people we look up to and want to emulate, even if we know nothing else about them. It's like calling a press conference to declare: "I like puppies!" Who cares? Everybody likes puppies. And we like delicious food, stunning works of art, sexy movie stars, rags-to-riches stories, and victorious athletes. We also like receiving praise when we win or succeed—giving the speech, graciously receiving the trophy, depositing the first big check after our raise. When someone coyly says, "Oh, stop!" what that person really mean is, "Don't you dare stop; this is what I live for!"

Jesus doesn't care about any of that, but we could hardly be more obsessed. Even in the Church world, we praise numerical growth, people who have turned their lives around, and religious celebrities. We're as shallow as anyone else—name one televangelist lacking charisma, or one religious leader who wouldn't eventually be shown the door if she didn't put butts in seats and cash in the coffers every Sunday. Beneath the veneer of religiosity, we are no different from popular culture. Church is just *American Idol,* but instead of pop music performances, we reward sermons full of manufactured drama and platitudes—and who could say no to a rousing gospel choir?

There is another peculiar kind of competition that is popular in American society beside competing to lavish praise on the praiseworthy. It is more popular than football or basketball; more popular than watching the train wrecks that are our national elections. More popular than *Survivor, X-Factor* and *Dancing with the Stars.*

You have seen and heard it on the news; you have read it on blogs and in your Facebook feed; you have been dragged into this competition whenever an argument comes up. The competition is simple—to find the ugliest thing. What is the worst natural disaster? Who is the most corrupt politician? Which party did the most to add to the deficit? What's worse—a Socialist, or a Birther, or a Neo-Conservative, or an Occupier? Who had the worst day? Who's got the worst boss?

The competition rears its head when we call each other Nazis[2] or Fascists, or when pundits on TV yell at each other from inside their boxes. It's when we tune in to reality TV to see who is going to

---

2. Godwin's law states, "As an online discussion grows longer, the probability of a comparison involving Nazis or Hitler approaches 1." Its corollary is that whoever makes the comparison automatically loses the debate and the discussion is ended. We really need to be more careful and creative with our analogies.

humiliate themselves tonight. It comes out at the bar when we start one-upping each other's horror stories and comparing scars. It's in those conversations when someone is telling you about something bad in their life, and you have nothing but the urge to say, "Oh yeah, well if you think that's bad, listen to this…"

For a society obsessed with youth and beauty, we sling a lot of ugliness at each other. Our relationship to beauty and success is no less broken than our relationship to ugliness and failure.[3] We respond to both in exactly the opposite way that Jesus did, and does. We love the winners and hate the losers, and we can't resist watching a race to the bottom. We treasure beauty that is not redeeming, and we revel in ugliness that is unredeemed.

Airbrushed Reality

NICK

Have you ever seen this video by Jesse Rosten: http://vimeo.com/34813864? *If not then put down this book, activate your browser, and watch it. I'll wait. It is his parody of every skin care, diet craze, or self-improvement commercial on television. "Fotoshop by Adobe" is representative of how in our culture our image of sexiness is artificial and manufactured, and therefore insulting to everyone.*

We spend our whole lives comparing ourselves to the images we see online and in magazines on a daily basis. We see something that is staged, crafted, and tweaked to match an idealized version of humanity. We think each new fad or craze will recraft us into that smoothed-out, blemish-cleared, color-enhanced, skinnier version of ourselves. We fall right into the praise trap of: "It's you, perfected!"

Every year at my church we host a "God's gift of sexuality" retreat for our seventh graders. We gather our students in one session and ask them to describe what the important qualities are about the opposite gender. Of course, the conversations starts off with looks and they pick images of celebrities out of magazines to embody this conversation. How many of these seventh grade girls look (or will ever look) like Megan

---

3. In the St Louis Cardinals' historic World Series run in 2011, David Freese was the Game 6 hero and eventual series MVP. Yet, even following his moment of triumph on the field, in a post-game interview he mentioned a dropped pop-up ball from the fifth inning. Even in the limelight, we obsess over our mistakes.

Fox? Particularly the images of Megan that were just trimmed out of the magazines by the boys? Even Megan Fox can't look like that Megan Fox. What this does to our self image, to our image of the world around us, to our view of what is praiseworthy, is undeniable. This isn't really praise at all; it's narcissism. We just want to see ourselves reflected back as that perfectly symmetrical light-skinned beauty, who we know deep down is just as fake as our society's beauty standards. As the video says, "Maybe she's born with it...ummm...no. I'm pretty sure it's Fotoshop."

All Things Dull and Ugly

When our praise is given to all the things people ordinarily value, then not only are we doing nothing remarkable, but we are also reinforcing the psychological and social mechanisms that create outcasts in the first place. We are just freshening the paint on the lines that divide the clean from the unclean, the worthy from the unworthy, the sacred from the profane. Meanwhile, Jesus is busy smearing those lines, or even erasing them altogether.

God is sometimes said to be impartial, drawing on Jesus' observation from nature that God causes the sun to rise on the evil *and* the good, and sends rain on the righteous *and* the unrighteous.[4] It would be better to say that God is intensely partial to *all* of creation. In the first creation account in the book of Genesis, God creates the universe day by day: dividing the light from the darkness, the water from the dry land, and breathing life into all the plants and animals. After each creative act, God declares the new addition "good." God finds goodness and takes delight in absolutely everything that exists—altogether, God calls it "very good."[5]

Matter matters. When the ancients who wrote this creation poetry tilted their heads back and contemplated the night sky, they were filled with the same kind of wonder we are when we gaze skyward. From the lowliest quark to the vast star nursery that gave birth to the furnace of energy and light that is our Sun, God loves everything. From the tiniest gnat to the gargantuan blue whale, God loves everything that lives and moves and simply is. God has blessed all of it and called it beautiful.

---

4. Matthew 5:45.
5. Genesis 1.

But when we look around us, we do not see a universe of undifferentiated goodness. We categorize things according to their utility or how they appeal to our senses. Thus we sing with the poet Cecil F. Alexander:

All things bright and beautiful,
All creatures great and small,
All things wise and wonderful,
The Lord God made them all
Each little flower that opens,
Each little bird that sings,
He made their glowing colours,
He made their tiny wings.

And so on... The lyrics continue, naming everything pleasing to the senses in nature, but excluding anything we would find distasteful—a fact that the geniuses at Monty Python noticed and parodied in their own theologically insightful song:

All things dull and ugly,
All creatures short and squat,
All things rude and nasty,
The Lord God made the lot
Each little snake that poisons,
Each little wasp that stings,
He made their brutish venom,
He made their horrid wings.

Everything that is listed in Monty Python's song belongs to the order of God's created goodness as much as the things that Mrs. Alexander chose to praise. All of it, according to God, is good. When we divide the world according to what is useful or pleasing to us versus what is inconvenient or disgusting to us, then we are dividing the good from the good. We are cutting ourselves and others off from the fullness of joy that God has prepared for us by despising things that God loves.

God's partiality toward all of creation is shown in that God's heart goes out to the rejected and despised in the world first. When we praise the grandeur of the mountains or the power of the sea, we aren't really praising God at all—we're praising our own ideals of strength and beauty. In order to praise God effectively, we must learn to appreciate all things "dull and ugly." We must learn to be, like God, partial to every part of the world, whether we find it personally pleasing or not.

Zen and the Art of Clinical Depression

DOUG

My whole life I've had low-grade depression, sometimes called dysthymia, as well as periodic bouts of more serious depression. If you've dealt with depression, you'll be familiar with the whirlpool of despair that sucks you down. If not, then imagine a crushing defeat you've felt in your life, or helpless and overwhelming grief, and then imagine feeling that way all the time. Imagine that your own mind is hijacked, and begins to continually reinforce those feelings by blowing bad things out of proportion, draining pleasure out of things you enjoy, and giving you the false intuition that this is all exactly what you deserve. These are all symptoms of depression, but in the midst of it, the afflicted person finds it almost impossible to see them as symptoms. The symptoms simply feel like self-evident truths.

I came to understand a very ancient principle from a Buddhist monk named Thich Nhat Hanh. He encourages "doing the dishes for the sake of doing the dishes." The idea is simple: imagine yourself doing the dishes, or some other mindless, repetitive, maybe dirty chore. As you do it, you're thinking, "Ugh, I hate doing the dishes. I wish I was doing something else. Where did all these freaking dishes come from?" And so on. Meanwhile, the dishes are still there. They aren't getting cleaned any faster—but you are making yourself needlessly unhappy while cleaning them.

If, however, you do the dishes for their own sake, trying to look at them appreciatively, not grumbling to yourself but just doing them calmly, accepting where you are and that sometimes dishes just have to get done, you find that the whole chore is a lot less aggravating. The dishes get done just as fast, if not faster, and you're happier at the end.

This idea of doing things for their own sake was a little shaft of light into my life. An expert at manufacturing my own misery, it was a necessary corrective. Over time, I found that I could apply this principle to the world around me—to other people, even to myself. Difficult, certainly, but worthwhile.

The idea that the cosmos is "very good" still goes against my intuition in every conceivable way. Deep down, I may always believe that the cosmos is an arbitrary Rube-Goldberg machine designed to manufacture misery. On the other hand, behaving as if the cosmos was very good, as if creation was wholly beautiful, doing things for their own sake and loving people for their own sakes, has done me nothing but good. It opens the possibility that perhaps I am even wrong about myself.

Chipped Ceramic

To train ourselves to appreciate things for their own sake, we have to undo the cultural baggage (and resist biological wiring) that teaches us to praise traits such as symmetry and being free of blemishes. We need to practice praising things for their imperfection and asymmetry. This is not merely overlooking the flaws in an object to find alternate appealing qualities, but actually praising the flaws themselves. We're not talking about sifting through the mundane till you find something exceptional, some diamond in the rough. We're talking about praising the mundane for its "mundanity."

There is a Japanese aesthetic sensibility that fits this concept well, called *wabi-sabi*. According to this worldview, nothing lasts, nothing is finished, and nothing is perfect. The transient, flawed quality of all existence is not seen as something to lament. Instead, something becomes more beautiful the more it evokes rough, natural simplicity. An old and wrinkled face is more beautiful than a youthful one, because wear and tear are not part of an inevitable decay over time from an initial state of perfection, but a progressive revelation of that person's true appearance.

From art to horticulture to architecture, this aesthetic of partiality to the mundane is expressed throughout Japanese society—most notably in the pottery used in Japanese tea ceremonies. Oftentimes the pottery has a very rustic and unremarkable appearance. The cups are asymmetrical. The color of the clay and the glaze is simple, perhaps in earth tones. There may be visible repairs or even chips on the bottom of the cups. For a practice enveloped in such elaborate ritual, the equipment at the center of the tea ceremony might seem disappointingly plain.

What isn't apparent unless you've been looking very closely at this same tea set for a long time is that a great deal of attention has gone into the appearance of these items. The chips on the bottom of those cups are intentional. Their asymmetrical shape is by design and requires a skilled potter to execute. The repairs have been left visible on purpose as a record of the history of that piece of pottery. That simple glaze? It changes color slowly, organically, over the course of decades as hot water is poured over the surface of the ceramic. The unique imperfections of the tea set are like the wrinkles on a person's face—telling you the story of its life.

We do *wabi-sabi* injustice, though, if we limit it to special objects where great care and attention has been put into their imperfection. The point of *wabi-sabi* is to train the participant to find the simplest, most common, and least important things fascinating, not in spite of their ordinariness, but because of their ordinary nature. A storm drain can be as interesting as a mountain top. A pile of trash probably has more stories to tell than a flowery meadow.

God showed a *wabi-sabi* aesthetic in picking the youngest of Jesse's sons, a simple sheep herder, to become the greatest and most beloved of Israel's kings.[6] God showed a *wabi-sabi* aesthetic in choosing a stable for a birthing room and a food trough for a cradle to hold the newborn king of kings.[7] Jesus showed a wabi-sabi aesthetic in choosing common things: water, bread, and wine to become the symbols of new life and the coming Kingdom.[8]

God loves the ordinary. In order to train ourselves to love the way God loves, we have to redirect our praise away from the perfect and instead toward the broken. We need to discover the beauty of cracked, flawed ceramic as well as blemished, asymmetrical people.

Don't Put That in Your Mouth

Perhaps you already see and praise the beauty of the ordinary, but there are things that no one would find attractive. There are things that deserve the label "ugly." There are things that disgust us outright. These are the things that can teach us the most about how to praise.

When we praise beauty and disparage ugliness, we are engaged in defining boundaries. We are saying, "That thing belongs over there" (away from me), and, "This thing belongs over here" (near me). The ability to separate our world into good and bad, useful and harmful, is important to human development. At the most basic level, our survival depends on us learning that certain things are good to eat, others not so much.

---

6. We refer to King David, of course, 1 Samuel 16:1–13.
7. Luke 2:1–20.
8. Luke 22:19–20; Matthew 28:19.

The emotional dynamic that causes you to react negatively to putting certain things in your mouth is what psychologists call *core* disgust. If we offered you a glass of lemonade with a cockroach floating in it, you would almost certainly decline. The feeling of disgust that may even arise in you from just the mention of a cockroach floating in your lemonade helps warn you that something is unsafe to eat. It is a powerful expulsive mechanism. We literally want to vomit, to push out, or expel the object of our disgust.

Humans, being omnivorous and adapted to living in a wide diversity of climates, need our core disgust to be adaptable and robust. In different regions there are different things that we shouldn't eat. None of us are born automatically knowing what we should avoid eating. Every parent has to tell a child at some point not to put something gross in its mouth. We must be taught in our early years what to regard as disgusting.

Because disgust is learned, it is psychologically promiscuous. Disgust attaches itself to things besides just what is unsafe or disgusting to eat. Disgust becomes an emotional boundary marker for social and moral judgments as well. At an early age in our culture, children become worried about "cooties." They label other children they don't like as "infected," and form exclusive social groups in which those rejected are considered disgusting.

As any child knows, cooties are contagious. The psychologist Richard Beck,[9] who has thought and written a great deal on issues of cleanliness and disgust on his blog and in his book Unclean, explains a critical trait of contagion: "negativity dominance." Negativity dominance means that when a clean and an unclean object come into contact the unclean object is stronger and pollutes the clean object: "The judgment of negativity dominance places all the power on the side of the pollutant. If I touch (apologies for the example I'm about to use) some feces to your cheeseburger the cheeseburger gets ruined, permanently... Importantly, the cheeseburger doesn't make the feces suddenly scrumptious. When the pure and the polluted come into contact the pollutant is the more powerful force. The negative

---

9. We really owe this whole section on disgust to Dr. Richard Beck's work, and many ideas elsewhere in this book were influenced by his always excellent blog Experimental Theology (http://experimentaltheology.blogspot.com/).

dominates the positive."[10] The cockroach ruins the lemonade—the lemonade does not redeem the cockroach.

What this means in a social context is that a person who has come to be a vector of contagion and impurity, someone whom we regard as disgusting, has to be expelled from the community forcefully, even violently. There can be no tolerance of the unclean person because any contact with this person results in you becoming unclean also. It is following the logic of disgust psychology that leads the Pharisee and the Levite in Jesus' parable about the good Samaritan to walk past without helping the injured man. If they come into contact with a stranger who may be unclean, touch unclean bodily fluids, or, worse, discover that the man is already a corpse—then they become unclean.[11]

What begins as social dynamics on the playground can quickly take on nefarious overtones. When children begin applying the psychology of disgust to their relationships, certain kids get isolated and targeted for peer abuse. Those deemed weird or ugly get tarred with insults that evoke purity distinctions. A hideous consensus quickly forms and few kids are willing to express dissent for fear that they will become the next targets of bullying. Associating with the outcast is social suicide. Far from being a benign phenomenon, bullying is increasingly recognized as a source of severe trauma for many children. Too often we have to read the testimonies of parents and teachers wishing they'd seen the signs earlier after a teenager has committed suicide, or homicide, due to bullying.[12]

The logic of disgust makes us do morally disgusting things. As a boundary marker, disgust gets forced into service maintaining false racial divisions. It is no accident that the language of White supremacy is the language of purity. As we subconsciously accept these distinctions, the target of our disgust becomes associated with every variety of impurity, from physical dirt and bad odors to supposed moral inferiority. Disgust imposes a metaphorical scale, in which

---

10. Richard Beck, *Unclean: Meditations on Purity, Hospitality, and Mortality* (Eugene, Oreg.: Cascade Books, 2011), 30.

11. Luke 10:25–37.

12. The effects of bullying last well into adulthood according to recent studies published in the Journal of JAMA Psychiatry (http://archpsyc.jamanetwork.com/article.aspx?articleid=1654916). Both victims of bullying and bullies were found to be far more likely to suffer from anxiety, depression, agoraphobia, and other mental illnesses as adults.

people who disgust us are less and less human, more animalistic, and even monstrous. As such we have no qualms about behaving in monstrous ways toward them.

At the absolute extreme this dynamic leads to genocide. The potent expulsive impulse of disgust has often been the engine of true horror. When a society demands purity, "ethnic cleansing" makes a terrifying kind of sense—it is the ultimate "cleansing" of impurities through horrific violence. What the psychology of disgust teaches us is that the seed of this kind of evil is in all of us. It depends on nothing more exotic than the intuition each of us has that some things are unclean, impure, and polluted.

Playground Warfare

ARIC

"You don't even know what a blowjob is? You're the dumbest faggot ever!" The girl, who was several grades ahead of me and much bigger, pushed me hard so I stumbled backward and fell down. The circle of her friends, all older and in my eyes terrifyingly large, laughed. Two of them kicked me, but I curled up so they hit me in the backpack and it only hurt a little bit. The kicks kept coming, though, and I couldn't block them all. I was seven years old.

This event started a period of my life lasting years, in which I ran to and from school as fast as I could by alternate routes, sneaking through people's backyards or hiding, sometimes for half-an-hour, in a bush, trying to avoid bullies. During recess I begged my teachers to be allowed to stay in the classroom. I never told them why, and they assumed I was just one of those shy or bookish kids, so they would force me to go out on the playground "for my own good." But the playground was a warzone for me.

I am a geek. I excelled academically in school, but I sucked (still do) at sports. I play role-playing games. I read a lot of science fiction and fantasy and can tell you more than you want to know about my favorite cult TV shows, movies, and comics. Nowadays and at my age this is more of a badge of pride than shame, but as a child in school it made me a target, and I was never smart enough to figure out how to change my image to avoid being bullied. It was not courage, trust me. If I could have done something to stop the bullying I would have. I would have done almost anything.

Before the bullying started, I had several good friends who lived in the same neighborhood as me. Once I had become a target they quickly learned that I was toxic. Not only did they quit playing with me, they joined in the bullying. "Fag" was the epithet they hurled most often, even though I had no idea what my sexuality was at that stage and neither did they. It didn't matter. The word didn't really mean "homosexual." It meant "disgusting"—which is exactly how they made me feel.[13]

Kissing Lepers

Hansen's disease, as we call leprosy now, is caused by a bacterium that is not very contagious and has a long incubation period, making it difficult to tell where and when a person became infected. It seems almost as if the disease came out of nowhere, an affliction from God. The most virulent form of this disease causes pale lesions and large nodules to appear on the skin. These early symptoms mark you as unclean, a source of contagion that has to be expelled from the community. Isolation and poverty increase your squalor and hasten the effects of the disease. In advanced stages it weakens your muscles and gradually decreases the sensitivity in your extremities. The numbness means that you are more prone to and often completely unaware of minor injuries, scrapes, and abrasions that happen to all of us. Unnoticed injuries get infected and turn gangrenous. After years, you are covered in decay as digits and limbs literally rot and fall away.

This is what was happening to the body of the man who approached Jesus in the fifth chapter of the Gospel according to Luke and threw himself on the ground, begging, "Lord, if you are willing, you can make me clean."[14] Understanding how disgust works, we can see that this is an absurd thing to say.

Disgust tends to be permanent. If we remove the cockroach from that glass of lemonade we offered you earlier, you still would not drink it. Even if we put the lemonade through a filter in front of you, you would probably reject the lemonade that once had the cockroach in it. Most people would continue to decline to drink the lemonade even if they were convinced that every last microscopic particle of cockroach had been removed. We irrationally believe that once the lemonade came into contact with the cockroach it was permanently

13. The piece of spoken word poetry "To This Day" by Shane Koyczan, found at the following web address, eloquently describes the experience of many who are bullied: http://www.youtube.com/watch?v=ltun92DfnPY.

14. Luke 5:12–16 (NIV).

tainted. Even if we forced ourselves to drink the lemonade, we would not enjoy it.

This man is claiming that Jesus can not only remove a bacterial infection and decades of putrefaction from his body, but also undo powerful, irreversible communal stigmas in a single act. Jesus ends up agreeing with this man that it is possible, and he wills the leper to be clean. The man's leprosy is healed, but this is not the miracle in the story. The miracle is what Jesus does before he says a word.

The first thing he does is reach out his hand and touch the man.

This is before Jesus has said, "Be clean!" and before Luke lets us know that the leprosy is healed. Jesus touches him *while he is unclean.* He touches the leper's suppurating wounds. He gets another man's puss and blood on his fingers. Because contagion is negativity dominant, this interaction should make Jesus unclean. When a clean (sacred) object comes into contact with an unclean (profane) object, the negative side always dominates. A filthy cockroach washed in clean lemonade doesn't make the cockroach suddenly pure. It's crazy to even suggest it. The cockroach pollutes the lemonade. But that isn't what happens when Jesus touches the leper. Jesus behaves as if he is (to borrow a term from Dr. Beck) *positivity dominant.* In the inverse of everything psychology and culture teach us, his touch makes the leper clean.

The presumption of positivity dominance extends to Jesus' disciples and the community that gathers in his name. His apostles performed the same sort of miracles, swimming against the stream of purity to touch lepers, the blind, the lame, Gentiles, prostitutes, tax collectors, and sinners of every variety. Early Christians were continually criticized for their table-fellowship practices, which brought them into close contact with the unclean—and they learned that table fellowship from Jesus. Again and again the gospels show us that, far from contaminating Jesus or his followers, these interactions led to the purification of the unclean.

Based on the example of Christ with the leper, many of the saints of Christian tradition have gone to great lengths to overcome their personal revulsion toward the unclean members of our society. St. Francis of Assisi as a young man from a wealthy family couldn't bear the disfigured, diseased individuals that lived outside his village. Along his path toward faithful discipleship he famously decided to go out to these people who he found disgusting and embrace them. He kissed the lepers. Catherine of Sienna took it even farther. While working in a hospital she overcame her aversion to treating the wounds of her patients by drinking a cup of pus.

The gospel presumption of positivity dominance extends to you as well. That which you embrace in love is purified.[15] If you praise what is ugly and despised, call clean what is filthy, and celebrate what no one desires, then you are doing more than speaking a counterintuitive truth— you are creating the reality you speak of. You have the power with words of authentic praise to incorporate someone who is outcast. Therefore, you are summoned by Jesus to live in defiance of the logic of disgust, to tear down the social and moral boundaries we erect between people, and to kiss the lepers clean.

He Had No Majesty

There is a final reason it is important for you to overcome your disgust, your culturally conditioned aesthetic values, and learn to praise what is rejected and unwanted: if you wish to praise Christ, this is the only way to do so.

Jesus knew something about ugliness—not the metaphorical "ugliness inside"—but the real cross-to-the-other-side-of-the-street kind of ugliness that means you never get that hot date or promotion. A few primarily Caucasian churches have grudgingly accepted the occasional depiction of Jesus as a person of color—which he obviously was—but he is still almost universally depicted as handsome. This is despite the fact that, while his appearance is never described in the gospels, the one spoken of in the prophecies of Isaiah is "lacking in majesty, and has no beauty such that we would desire him."[16]

Jesus was ugly. Or, at the very least, the one predicted by Isaiah was described as unappealing, and some of the people who met Jesus seemed to feel that he was the fulfillment of those old prophecies.

---

15. Love transforms and redeems our perceptions, whether we want it to or not. If you have ever fallen in love, you may recall one of the effects that it has: faults that in others would aggravate you in your beloved seem almost endearing. When we truly love people, we love them for their own sakes, not because of what they can do for us, or because of how they make us look or how they make us feel.

16. Author paraphrase of Isaiah 53:2.

Certainly, no one took the time to mention that Isaiah was wrong about his looks. In the very best-case scenario, Jesus was homely—nothing in his appearance was worthy of comment, and he was not desirable to look at.

More than just having an ugly face, Jesus' life was repulsive. He called people away from safety and security, prestige and public approval. He told his disciples they must hate their families, refuse to cling to material possessions, and not even to seek pride in spiritual superiority. He started his career with crowds of thousands listening to his teachings, and he drove them all away with his strident, unappealing message until even his closest and most trusted friends betrayed and abandoned him to his enemies.

All the while, this ugly Jesus was spending a great deal of time among ugly people, loving them and healing them and calling them clean even when they were filthy in every sense of the word.[17] Jesus the ugly brought good news to the ugly, the unclean, and the unwanted. He chose them and loved them and associated with them most closely. He was utterly uninterested in what anyone thought of those whose tables he shared, or whether his refusal to incessantly wash his hands was disgusting in anyone's eyes.

Jesus the ugly Christ died an ugly death, and was buried. He rose up, still bearing the ugly wounds, and returned to our world and calls out to those who are ugly, unwanted, and unclean with words of purest praise: "You are beautiful; you are loved; my life is your life."

***

Wayne slipped his surgical mask up over his nose before pushing the door open. The warm odor of feces was strong, but he kept a smile in his eyes as he asked the nurse how he could assist her. She handed him soiled clothes and sheets to bag. Together they helped Mrs. Brandt out of the bed and over to the shower, lowering her onto a stool. While the nurse gave Mrs. Brandt a shower, Wayne cleaned the room, taking the pungent trash all the way out to the dumpster. Since he had started volunteering at the assisted living facility, he had seen some ugly parts of life he'd never contemplated before, but the chance to love and care for those who were forgotten and brushed aside was beautiful.

---

17. For a modern-day interpretation of this, you might explore what some psychologists might call "unconditional positive regard."

Experiments in Praise

■ Find something ugly—really ugly—at a flea market or garage sale or online. We're talking dead plant, painting of dogs playing poker on black velvet, or piece of clashing furniture from the 1970s. Put the ugly thing in your home and when you have people over, make sure you mention how much you like it and how beautiful it is. Enjoy the looks of confusion and discomfort on your friends' faces as they try to decide what to say.

■ Volunteer somewhere that you have to put your hands on stuff that grosses you out –spend time at a garbage dump sorting trash that can be recycled; clean someone else's toilet. Work somewhere that you may come in contact with bodily fluids such as at an assisted living facility, with the developmentally disabled, or with people experiencing homelessness.

■ Take unflattering pictures of yourself. Tape the pictures around your mirror, or on the underside of your sun visor in your car, or inside your computer case. Whenever you see the pictures, however you feel, you have to say something like, "Hey there, beautiful," "Yowza!" or, "It's always great to see you." Do this until you mean it.

■ Don't dress unprofessionally for work, but dress down. Wear some bland clothing; don't do anything special with your hair; wear only basic makeup. Grow out a little stubble. Observe whether people treat you differently as a result. To up the ante, call them on it.

Confess!

Angela is finally ready to confess. She sits in her pew, head bowed while the music plays, and sheds silent tears. She thinks of the people she has wronged, the mistakes she has made; she gathers up all she has done wrong, or left undone, and gives it all to God. She asks for God's forgiveness, and a feeling of peace flows into her. Now she is free—it suddenly feels like those things never happened.

Wasting God's Time

When most Christians think of confession, they imagine admitting their sins to God through a priest, in private, or in corporate worship, so that they may be forgiven. How often does this work as a placebo, making us feel better about our wrongdoing while letting us weasel out of actually facing the people we've hurt and let down, hearing from them what we've done, and trying to make amends? If I hurt you, then go to church and confess my sin to God (silently, of course) and experience a feeling of forgiveness, what does this mean to you? Nothing. You're still hurt and I still haven't faced up to what I did.

On the other hand, say I hurt you, and then when I realize what I've done. I come to you and say what I've done, ask for you to say anything I might have missed, truly hear you when you say how it impacted you, apologize and ask what I can do to make amends. I follow through with making amends, and do what it takes to earn the trust that I'd lost. Amidst all this, I fail to go to church and silently confess to God so that I can feel that peaceful sensation of forgiveness.

In the first case, my concern is that I feel better, and I use God to help me feel better, despite doing nothing to make things right. In the other case, my concern is with what I did to you, and in hearing you say what you need to say to me, while not justifying my actions, but rather doing what I can to make amends for what I did. Why does the church talk so much about the first kind of confession and less about the second? It's easy to waste God's time with confession that will not amount to a change in our actual relationships. Talking to God is too often an emotional placebo, making us feel better, but not making us better people.

Placebo confession works for anesthetizing our conscience, partially because we have accepted the falsehood that there is a divide between the internal world of thoughts and emotions and the external world of behaviors and consequences. Our tendency is to prioritize the interior world as the seat of identity. We may behave reprehensibly, but inside we still feel like good people and we cling to what we think of as our noble motives.[1]

As an example, imagine you overhear a couple friends laughing about a racist joke. You approach them and point out that the joke was racist. They immediately respond by saying, "We're not racist!" and cite relationships and anecdotes in their own defense. You tried to initiate a conversation about external behaviors, but it quickly became a conversation about internal identity. So long as that firewall between behavior and identity exists, there's almost no way to reach someone in a conversation like this. They think that who they are and how they feel on the inside is more important than what they say and do.[2]

Too many of us have been told that it is what is on the inside that counts. As a result, we engage in pious habits that keep our conscience from troubling us, but often have little or no impact on the way we behave toward others. It's time we recognized that there is no division between our interior world and the people around us. How we behave *is* what we believe and what we do *is* who we are. In order to confess, truly confess, we have to be transformed from the outside in. Or, as James puts it in his epistle, "Faith without works is

---

1. Consider our discussion of a "robot army" in "Awaken!"
2. Jay Smooth gave an excellent talk at TEDx at Hampshire College on November 15, 2011 (http://www.youtube.com/watch?v=MbdxeFcQtaU) in which he suggested that we accustom ourselves to thinking of racism like dental hygiene. No one takes it personally when they're told they have something stuck in their teeth. They just go clean their teeth. Similarly, when we learn something we've just said was racist, we could just take it as an opportunity to clean up our speech.

dead."[3] To treat confession as more than a "get out of jail free card" requires two things: self-knowledge and accountability.

Art and Socrates

According to Plato, the great philosopher Socrates often encouraged and even rebuked his students with the words: "Know thyself." Self-knowledge is no gift of the gods, but is won by struggle. It was the inscription described as gracing the entrance to the Temple of Apollo at Delphi, and has been attributed to any number of philosophers and poets since. It is hard to find a philosophy or religion that does not take self-knowledge to be, at the very least, a central concern, if not *the* central concern and source of wisdom. In order to be moral, Peter Abelard said, one must know oneself first.[4] The results of a lack of self-knowledge can range from the humorous to the disastrous, depending on the situation and the stature and influence of the person involved.

Though chasing down a particular definition of art can be difficult even for philosophers, a core concern of art and the artist is self-knowledge. The poet who shapes the poem, the sculptor who frees the image from stone, the painter who layers color—all are well-served by self-knowledge, and all seek to express something of themselves in their work. Programs such as The Artist's Way are aimed at increasing self-understanding as a way to improve one's artistic expression.[5] Creating art can deepen people's knowledge of themselves, and the experience and study of art can itself lead to greater understanding.

The practice of confession begins with the kind of self-knowledge found in both philosophers and artists, because any kind of confession, from credo to repentance, is impossible if we do not first know ourselves. Imagine a parent whose small child has done something wrong but doesn't know why he or she did it. The parent will often cajole the child into apologizing, but before a certain developmental point (which for some never comes at all), children don't really understand why they've done what they've done, much less why

---

3. James 2:14–26 Paraphrase (NASB).
4. Peter Abelard (1079–1142) was a logician and philosopher of the middle ages. His treatise Know Yourself details a moral theory beginning with an understanding of one's intentions.
5. Julia Cameron, *The Artist's Way: A Spiritual Path to Higher Creativity,* (New York: Jeremy P. Tarcher/Putnam; 10nth anniversary edition, 2002).

something is wrong. The impulse comes, and without reflection or pause, a child acts on it.

This is perfectly appropriate for small children, and is utterly disastrous for adults, particularly those of us trying to live a Christian life. Without self-knowledge, we cannot know how to change or when to make amends or whom we ought to be. Without self-knowledge, we do not know why we do what we do, and we just blunder through life, sometimes hurting and sometimes helping, but baffled as to how it all fits together. People seem angry, and we can't figure out why—or we know we've hurt them, and feel bad about it, but we keep hurting them nonetheless.

Self-knowledge, in the way we usually mean it, does not seem to have been a preoccupation among the various biblical peoples. Navel-gazing is pretty much absent from the stories of Abraham, Moses, Esther, and the Prophets. With Jesus, though, we see what seems like a concern for self-knowledge. In the synoptic gospels we have a Jesus who immediately after he is baptized goes out into the wilderness to be tested. In Jesus' wilderness testing, he learns more about himself, and we learn more about him.

Will he use his divine power and status to relieve his discomfort and hunger? No. Will he claim rulership over the world in a demonic fashion, choosing power over others from on high if it is offered? No. Will he call upon the heavenly host to rescue him from danger or harm? No. We can never know what Jesus' ministry would have been like if he had never had this testing early on, but we can assume that everything Jesus did, he felt was necessary. So, even for Jesus, it was necessary to go out into the desert, alone and without comforts, and to come face to face with his deepest temptations.[6] Can we do less, if we are going to follow him?

The comparison with Jesus will of course not be flattering. Most of us have not been hungry for four days, much less forty days—who knows what we'd do to get some food at that point? And who hasn't begged for God to save them from danger, or hasn't salivated at the opportunity to be put in charge of everything for once? But the principle stands: before we go out into the world, making proclamations and trying to make things right, we need to understand ourselves as deeply as we can.

---

6. Matthew 4:1–11; Mark 1:12–13; Luke 4:1–13.

Learning hurts

NICK

Have you ever been in a situation in which you learned way more about what you do than you ever wanted to know? In Clinical Pastoral Education (a process that most mainline pastors go through before ordination) a tool exists that does exactly that; it's called Inter-Personal-Relations, or IPR. Essentially it's a group process by which you and your peers sit down in a room and tell each other what impact everything you said and did this week had on each of you.

Picture yourself sitting in Golden Gate Park after a delightful stroll with your CPE peer group during your second week on the job. The sun is shining, the grass is a bright green, the sweet fragrance of the fresh flowers is in the air. You all sit down to enter into your first IPR session as a group underneath a large redwood tree. Then each member of your group proceeds to tell you that every way that you attempted to help them each this week actually disempowered them to do those tasks, and that the more you try to help the more it just makes them feel like you're telling them the way you do something is the only right way to do it. You managed to push them around and belittle them by being in their face all week, and you tended to do it with a look that they were all reading as smugness.

Yep, that was my first IPR session. It was a giant confessional booth for me right there in the middle of Golden Gate Park, sitting under that large redwood. I sat at the center of the group painfully learning how my extroversion and overfunctioning really doesn't help anyone, including me. In fact, the more I did it, the less I learned. Right there in that park, I experienced the first group in my life willing to tell me the truth about myself...and it hurt.

Wasting Each Other's Time

The Catch-22 of self-knowledge is that there is no one on earth who has more practice and skill at lying to you than you. Accurate self-knowledge is the holy grail of mental health partly because it is so elusive. Whether you are more prone to arrogant self-aggrandizement or despairing self-deprecation, it is likely that you haven't told the truth about yourself to yourself very often in your life. Worst of all, our ability to deceive ourselves is sophisticated enough that, even when we think we're taking an honest appraisal of our lives, it is almost impossible to tell if we're correct.

We have this stereotype of a person on a journey of self-discovery: traveling to unfamiliar places; spending a lot of time in solitude; writing in a journal; staring wistfully at the night sky, or a landscape, or into the mirror. It's all very introspective and it's wildly misleading. There is value to a change of scenery. We can and do get stuck in ruts that obscure the truth about our lives from ourselves. Nevertheless, the most valuable learning you can do about yourself comes in the context of a group of people willing to hold you accountable by speaking the truth about you to your face. It is community, not solitude, that offers our best opportunity to know ourselves.

The church is in a position to be that community of accountability, but while the church talks a great game about confession, in practice we're terrible at it. At the heart of most churches is a widespread collusion to refrain from telling the truth, keep our true selves (and doubts and feelings) hidden while we confess to God rather than to each other, "repent" but never actually change our behavior,[7] and "get saved" over and over again without ever being saved *from* anything.

There are a lot of pitfalls to avoid when trying to create a community of accountability. In an authoritarian environment, accountability becomes another word for control. Where there is unequal disclosure or where people are held to different standards, we just create another opportunity for gossip and judgment. No one can be exempt from the process of discernment and truth-telling, and often special effort must be made to ensure that people who belong to disenfranchised groups or nondominant cultures have every opportunity to participate and be heard.

For a community of accountability to succeed it must be built on trust and equality. Ideally it will be a small group of people who share a commitment to honesty and support—where judgment is withheld, but members are bold about exposing their own struggles and inadequacies. In such an environment it is possible to begin to know oneself well enough to live with integrity. It won't be a comfortable process, but it is the road to truth. For those who claim to follow the Way, the Truth, and the Life,[8] nothing less will do. Lets not waste time lying to ourselves or to each other.

---

7. The irony being that to "repent" means literally to turn around.
8. John 14:6.

Den of LIES

DOUG

One of the things I like least about church is that it is a den of lies. I say that because the single thing that probably takes more time and energy in church than anything else, including everything that a pastor does, is making it so we appear to each other as if we are okay. I have heard countless stories of people in the midst of tremendous suffering going to church week after week, in every way playing the part of the faithful member and volunteer, all the while knowing that they can never actually talk about their pain, their doubt, their anger, or their fear.

The idea is as simple as it is insidious: if we are in good with God, our lives should be comfortable. If we suffer, then that is a sign that we are not in good with God. It's like being in the middle of a school of piranhas—church people can smell blood in the water, and will not hesitate to bite. On any given Sunday, the church sanctuary is a sea of blandly smiling faces and hidden agonies. In the pulpit things are even worse—that's the ringleader, the alpha piranha, whose complicity keeps everyone suffering alone and in silence. Pastors know that to express doubt can mean losing one's job, and every pastor wants to be the grinning leader of a flourishing congregation in which nothing goes wrong because everyone loves Jesus in the correct way.

To be in relationship with God and with each other, in church and elsewhere, means being who we actually are: faltering, angry, afraid, questioning messes stumbling our way through life hoping that no one notices. This is a matter of integrity, and it begins with whoever the leaders are. As leaders we must be willing to fail in public, to ask our questions out loud, to talk about when we are hurt or sad or angry or afraid. The privilege of the position of church leadership enables us to lie to ourselves and others far too easily, and we need to stop doing that. If we don't have the courage to do that, we can't possibly expect anyone we're supposedly serving to be honest with us, nor with each other.

Fail big, and be the mess in public that you know you are in private. Or, if you really are that put together, then what the heck are you doing in church?

Yes Means Yes

There is another kind of confession, sometimes called a *credo*, which is simply a term for when we tell the truth about ourselves, who we are, and what we think. Doing this authentically requires a particular approach to the words "yes" and "no." What Jesus had to say about these two words was very simple: don't swear by anything, but let your yes be yes, and your no be no, because anything other than that comes from the evil one.[9]

We see this principle illustrated when someone on television takes the stand in a courtroom, places a hand on the Bible, and swears to "tell the truth, the whole truth, and nothing but the truth, so help me God," or when we hear people exclaim, "I swear to God!" as a way to emphasize the truth of what they're describing. If you think about it, these statements are only necessary for someone who isn't a trustworthy person—and if the person isn't trustworthy to begin with, do we really think that placing a hand on a Bible or invoking God's name will make the person honest? What Jesus is saying is that if we have to make elaborate promises or swear oaths when we speak in order to convince people we are telling the truth, this means we aren't trustworthy to begin with. If we are known to have integrity and to tell the truth, then the swearing and promising seems superfluous. As disciples, we are supposed to be the kind of trustworthy people who are as good as our word.

This causes more trouble than we might think. There are times we say yes or no in order to get along and to avoid trouble or social discomfort. There are times we agree to something we don't really want to do and that we don't intend to work very hard at. There are times when we tell people what they want to hear because if we're honest, we might upset them, or lose our standing. This is especially common, again, in church. There are a lot of "official" things that a church will say everyone believes, but then you talk to the people and if they're honest with you, they'll tell you that they don't believe various parts of the supposedly non-negotiable dogma. It would just be so much trouble to be honest, and they don't want to be kicked out of their community because they don't quite line up the way they're supposed to.

A life of integrity, however, in which we are known to be honest and reliable people, is a lot simpler. When we speak, we are believed. When we say yes, we are trusted. When we say no, we are heard. Anyone might have a lot of friends and acquaintances, but the most

9. Matthew 5:37; James 5:12.

important friend, the deepest relationship, is with the person who will tell you the truth. Without that person in our lives, we are lost.

Telling the truth gives everything we say more power. Compare something Martin Luther King Jr. said to something a modern politician or TV pundit might say. Whose words do we trust? Whose words carry more power? What someone like Martin Luther King Jr. says is powerful because he was known to tell the truth, even the very painful truth we don't want to hear, and even at great personal cost. The words of a truth-teller carry much more weight than those of someone we know to be untrustworthy. Even after such truthful people die, their words still ring with power, because we know the integrity that they had. We know how rare and precious that integrity is, because we know how hard it is for us to tell the truth—to let our yes simply be yes, and our no simply be no.

When we tell the truth about ourselves and what we believe, that is a *credo*. The true credo, the confession of faith, arises out of our integrity. If your yes means anything but yes, or your no means anything but no, then your credo is worth almost nothing. But the confession of someone with integrity, a truth-teller, can change the course of history, and inspire people to greatness. That integrity begins with, and is founded on, yes and no.

A Man of Scruples

ARIC

Publicly confessing who you are and what you believe is a risky enterprise. In my religious tradition, when a person seeks membership in a new community that person is asked to make a confession of faith. Often this is treated as a mere formality, but when earnest disagreement arises (as it often does) we have a procedure we call "scrupling," in which that individual can declare his or her departure from the official doctrine or practice of the community. When this happens the community then debates whether that person's "scruple" is too serious a divergence for him or her to be welcomed as a member, or whether it is a tolerable exercise of freedom of conscience.

When I was seeking ordination as a minister, I submitted a scruple stating that I disagreed with the church's then-official standard that only married heterosexuals or celibate individuals were eligible for ordination. I did so with fear and trembling and against the advice of almost everyone whom I respected.

"Just duck your head. Don't make waves. Lay low and get yourself ordained. There will be time for standing on principle afterward," they told me.

I really was sorely tempted not to scruple. Being a married heterosexual man, the church's policy didn't directly affect me. If I just kept my mouth shut, my ordination would occasion no controversy. But contemplating keeping silent made me sick to my stomach. The sticking point for me were friends who were unjustly barred from ordination by this policy, friends who did not have the luxury of just keeping their heads down and hoping to escape notice. How could I claim to be in solidarity with them if I was conveniently silent when faced with personal risk?

So I submitted my statement and prepared myself for the debate that would decide the future of my vocation. Years of seminary, an international move, the immediate financial well-being of my family—it was all bound up in my confession.

Forced Confession

A vivid image of "forced confession" comes from the Bond film *Goldfinger*. James Bond is strapped to a table and a laser is slowly cutting along the table, poised to slice him in half. Bond sees this and demands of Goldfinger, "You expect me to talk?" Goldfinger laughs and replies, "No, Mr. Bond, I expect you to die!" For James Bond, it is a reasonable assumption—if a villain is threatening to cut him in half with a huge laser, it must be a way to get him to reveal information. This must be a forced confession. Goldfinger seems to have predicted this response. Of course James Bond will assume there is a way out, that he is not about to be killed. At this point in the film, however, Goldfinger couldn't care less what Bond has to say. He just wants to drag out his death a bit to increase the suffering involved—and unwittingly, of course, to give Bond the opportunity to make his escape so that the story can continue.

In the United States, our relationship with forced confession has changed drastically in the wake of the September 11th attacks. Before 9/11, torture was something that villains did. We would expect it from someone like Goldfinger, because he's an evil bastard who hurts people for fun and to achieve selfish ends. After 9/11, however, we have become a lot more like Goldfinger. Perhaps we do not hurt people for fun, but we are now willing to hurt them for information.

This is not only an issue in discussions of waterboarding on the news, or horrific stories about the treatment of prisoners at Guantanamo Bay, or the cavalier attitude of the former Vice President and Secretary of Defense with regard to "enhanced interrogation techniques," We can see this sea-change reflected in popular culture as well. On the television show *24*, Jack Bauer was regularly called upon to engage in "forced confession," threatening and torturing people in order to find the truth and save the day. Not only does the U.S. government now engage in practices for which it executed people as war criminals in the past, but we have turned to torture for entertainment and edification. U.S. culture has bought into the idea that the way to get at the truth, quickly and reliably, is to threaten and torture someone.

This is in contrast to the demonstrated fact, well-known among professional interrogators, that torture fails in its stated goals. A person being tortured is not motivated to offer information or tell the truth. A person being tortured is motivated to do and say whatever will make the torture stop. What results from torture, apart from the utter moral failure of the torturer and the lasting enmity of the victim, are eagerly offered lies and half-truths. This is not merely a moral distinction, but a factual one. Ali Soufan, a former FBI interrogator, does not believe that torture itself is intrinsically wrong. It is simply his experience that torture does not work. In Senate testimony, the interrogator who obtained a confession from multiple terror suspects without torture claimed that waterboarding, far from increasing actionable intelligence, caused the useful information to dry up.[10]

Our image, therefore, of "forced confession" is entirely the product of fiction, both in entertainment and in politics. Nonetheless, every one of us is in the midst of a forced confession of sorts. Whether

---

10. The testimony of Ali Soufan, given on May 13, 2009, is available in a complete transcript on the Senate Judiciary site (http://www.judiciary.senate.gov/). It is a small part of an overwhelming tide of evidence proving that torture is almost always ineffective. On December 14, 2012, the Senate Intelligence Committee approved a three-year-long study of "harsh interrogation techniques," concluding they were entirely ineffective (http://articles. washingtonpost.com/2012-12-13/world/35812850_1_harsh-interrogation-measures-network-of-secret-prisons-coercive-interrogation). Neuroscientists have demonstrated in laboratory experiments that stress and pain work directly against the mechanisms our brain uses to recall information and tell the truth (http://www.thedailybeast.com/newsweek/2009/09/21/the-tortured-brain.html). Arguments in favor of torture need to be put to rest: not only is torture an utter moral failure, it is counterproductive as well.

we want it to be or not, our life is our confession, and no amount of anti-interrogation training can change this fact. Rather, it is the result of what we might call "forced integrity." Or, as Jesus might put it, "the good person brings forth good things out of the good stored up in the heart, and the evil person brings forth evil out of the evil in the heart, because out of the overflow of the heart the mouth speaks."[11]

Goldfinger doesn't need a laser; Dick Cheney doesn't need a water board; we are human and who we are shows in what we say and do. Our life is our confession, whether we want it to be or not. What you say and do every day speaks louder than any admission or declaration that you could make. If we fail to trust people, then we are distrustful. If we make shady business deals to get ahead, then we are dishonest. If we never do what we say we are going to do, then we have no integrity. This is clear regardless of what we write on a job application or in our Twitter bios.

God's Confession, and Ours

For Christians, God's confession is Jesus. This is true on a number of levels: we see Jesus as embodying what God wishes to express to us. Jesus is the medium who is also the message.[12] In that we see Jesus as God, we also see who God is mostly clearly in Jesus, in the same way that in looking at our actions, other people can see most clearly who we are on the inside. Jesus is God's credo as well as God's definitive act.

It is impossible to know the mind or intentions of God. It isn't even possible to be certain about the thoughts and intentions of other human beings. We have to ask them, and then decide whether we believe them, based on their actions. Plenty of people want to tell us what God thinks, or what God intends. The best we are able to do, as a way of discerning, is to look at the stories we have of what Jesus said and did, and let those reveal God's character and what God values.

We can look at Jesus' refusal to retaliate, even in self-defense, and we have some evidence that God does not intend us to resort to violence. We can see that Jesus was well-known for sharing a table with outcasts, the unclean, and people known to be sinners, and so

---

11. Author paraphrase of Luke 6:45.
12. The seminal work by Marshall McLuhan on this, *Understanding Media: The Extensions of Man* (London: Sphere Books, 1967), famously proclaimed: "The Medium is the Message."

we can infer that God does not value those clean/unclean distinctions that we put so much energy into enforcing. We can read stories of Jesus healing, and perhaps decide that God intends for us to be whole and restored to our purpose. We can see that Jesus formed a traveling community around himself, and conclude that God intends for us to live in community. We can see Jesus asking forgiveness for those who tortured him and were in the midst of killing him, and draw from this that God intends for us to forgive even the unforgivable.

This is not a perfect process, but it is probably the best one we have for understanding another person, including persons about whom we only have stories. This confession of God can help us illuminate difficult things we might hear about God. If someone claims that God wants us to hurt other people, or exclude people on supposedly moral grounds, or seek revenge, or look to our own safety at the expense of others, or cooperate with Empire, we can have some confidence refusing to do so, because we have God's confession in Jesus.

For our confession, we have any number of words we might say to ourselves, to each other, and to God, but our truest confession is the same as the best confession we have of God—our confession is what we do. Who we are and what we do have what we might call an "intrinsic integrity." Despite our best efforts at deception, the truth comes out. The peace lover who finds ways to wound others, the pastor who steals from the congregation, the banker who gambles other people's retirement for his own gain, the supposedly loving matriarch who holds lifelong grudges—whatever these people tell us, their actions speak to us, loud and clear.

If we find that we continually do things we feel guilty about, or ashamed of, or have to apologize for, or hide from others, the problem is that we are not who we think we are. Losing self-control is more like losing self-deception. Psychologists such as Freud and Jung spoke about this as having a "Shadow," a part of ourselves that we try to ignore and repress. This shadow comes out, however, unconsciously and outside our control. The only choice is to seek to understand what we try to hide from ourselves and others, to come to grips with who we actually are.[13]

---

13. Consider Doug's aside *A Wizard of Earthsea* (spoiler alert) in the chapter "Love!"

But that is not enough. Confession is not merely an automatic process over which we have no control. The process works in the opposite direction as well—our actions change who we are on the inside. C.S. Lewis noted this process in *Mere Christianity*,[14] and it has been demonstrated experimentally,[15] that our actions can alter our perceptions, our thoughts, and even our brains. We build who we are from the outside in.

This gives even more weight to our confession. Saying who we are bears no weight whatsoever if it contradicts what we do. On the other hand, what we do becomes who we are. It is possible for us to do more than just act out what we try to repress and then frantically seek to hide it from others. We can choose a better, more difficult way. We can live as the kinds of people we want to be in truth, until at last we find that we are who we were striving to be.

Just as we know of God through Jesus and the stories we have of what Jesus did, we know ourselves, and make ourselves known to others through what we do. This can be a very painful, shame-inducing process of acting out and then hiding, an ongoing spiral of self-deception and even self-hatred; or it can be far simpler—we can, to a degree, choose who we are. We can choose to confess, with our lives, what it is we think we should be able to confess with our lips. We can have true integrity—we can fit together as a whole—by honestly being who we are, and then courageously being who we are meant to be.

***

Paul felt like he was going to vomit. He already had vomited once, in

---

14. "Do not waste time bothering whether you 'love' your neighbor; act as if you did. As soon as we do this we find one of the great secrets. When you are behaving as if you loved someone, you will presently come to love him. If you injure someone you dislike, you will find yourself disliking him more. If you do him a good turn, you will find yourself disliking him less. There is, indeed, one exception. If you do him a good turn, not to please God and obey the law of charity, but to show him what a fine forgiving chap you are, and to put him in your debt, and then sit down to wait for his 'gratitude,' you will probably be disappointed. (People are not fools: they have a very quick eye for anything like showing off, or patronage.) But whenever we do good to another self, just because it is a self, made (like us) by God, and desiring its own happiness as we desire ours, we shall have learned to love it a little more or, at least, to dislike it less." C.S. Lewis, *Mere Christianity*, (San Francisco: Harper San Francisco, 2009), ch. 9.

15. Even virtual behavior can make a person more empathetic: http://news.stanford.edu/news/2013/january/virtual-reality-altruism-013013.html

fact. In the next room his family and a few of his closest friends waited for him to explain why he had asked them all to come over. When he thought of the pain that he had caused all of them by his dishonesty, and the pain it would cause them now for him to finally tell the truth, it was like being stabbed. Most of all he feared losing their affection once everything was in the open. But there was no choice. To continue to uphold this lie would only do more harm to everyone, including him. Whatever it cost, Paul knew that he was willing to pay it in order to be able look at himself in the mirror again.

Experiments in Confession

■ Attend a meeting of AlAnon, AlaTeen (if you are a teen), AA, or another 12-step group, either as a supportive observer, or because you actually have an issue in your life you're struggling with. Watch how people confess. If you have the guts, and you have something to say, stand up and say it when there is a moment.

■ Pretend you are a private investigator hired to figure out what you value. Go through your garbage, your fridge, phone record, Internet search history, bank records, everything. Write down the big things that keep coming up in your life. How do you spend your time and money and energy? When you're done, look at what you learned, and consider whether this is the life you want.

■ If you go to church or have another kind of regular religious or spiritual practice, next time, in a way that is appropriate to your community, confess. If you have the courage, confess to everyone, but at least to a leader. You don't have to confess everything, but confess something. After, think about whether you feel better or worse, having done that.

■ Commit to a "Week of Honesty." During this Week, you will only say yes when you mean yes, and no when you mean no. You can be sly about it, and say things such as, "I don't want to answer that," but you can't say a single thing you know to be untrue. At the end of the Week of Honesty, commit to another Week of Honesty.

Expel!

Worship has long since ended, but there is still a knot of activity at the altar at the front of the sanctuary. Nate kneels in the middle of a circle of people, tears falling, crying out to God. He is surrounded by the pastor, music director, and a number of the church's most ardent spiritual warriors. They make petitions to God, they speak in tongues, and lay their hands on Nate's shoulders and head. The demons are rooted deep in Nate, and they know it, because they do this almost every week.

Unbelieving

From the perspective of the authors of this book, and we're willing to bet many of our readers, we no longer live in a demon-haunted world. We are not concerned whether someone in our town has the power of the evil eye. We do not have to seek out witch-finders in order to discover who it is that is hexing us and causing our illness or bad luck. When we talk about "discerning spirits,"[1] we're speaking metaphorically. We're probably talking about discerning ideas, or discerning intuitions perhaps—but intuitions in the philosophical sense of observations or perceptions we cannot account for, rather than intuition in the sense of a third eye or extra-sensory perception.

When people talk about demons, we assume that what they mean is something like mental illness, but they don't have the terminology to identify what's *really* going on. Or maybe what they mean when they say demons is that there are things in their pasts that they'd rather not talk about in polite company, things they have done, or things

---

1. 1 Corinthians 12:10; 1 John 4:1–6.

49

that were done to them, that have lingering effects long after the fact. Or when they talk about demons, they might mean that there are parts of themselves that they don't like, or that they don't have conscious control over—urges or addictions.

In western society, most people do not believe in demons, and yet many of these same unbelievers will tell you a story about a loved one narrowly escaping a dangerous situation and attribute it to the work of a "guardian angel." The theologian Walter Wink has some words for this selective spirituality: "It is comforting to believe we are all protected by guardian angels, for example. But these guardian angels seem to work best in middle-class neighborhoods where there are plenty of resources; they don't do so well protecting children in ghettos from drive-by shootings. If we want to take the notion of angels [and] demons seriously, we will have to go back to the biblical understanding of spirits in all its profundity and apply it freshly to our situation today."[2]

A robust understanding of spirits means looking at the practice of exorcism in scripture, when for many of us exorcism has become the stuff of fantasy. Far from being a useful skill, we only see it in horror films about the power of supernatural evil being faced down by brave priests in liturgical collars wielding ancient rites and trembling rosaries. What does a postmodern, pluralistic, technological society like ours have to do with exorcism? At first glance, nothing at all.

The problem with this unbelief is that Jesus did a lot of exorcising. Demons and demonic possession figure prominently in the story of his life and ministry. Many of his healings were exorcisms: casting out demons. Would Jesus spend all this time on something meaningless to us now? At the very beginning of the Gospel according to Mark, Jesus is in the synagogue in Capernaum on the Sabbath when a demon-possessed man cries out, "What do you want with us, Jesus of Nazareth? Have you come to destroy us? I know who you are— the Holy One of God!" Jesus immediately orders him to be quiet and drives the spirit out of him. The crowd watching this scene is confused and begins to ask what kind of teacher this man from Nazareth is, and from where he gets his authority.[3]

2. Walter Wink, *The Powers That Be* (New York: Doubleday, 1998), 23.
3. Mark 1:21–28.

A lot of the people who met Jesus didn't understand who he was. Even when he took pains to explain clearly, most people refused to recognize him. Yet, Jesus was known all too well by the demons in the text. When Jesus faced off with these demons, exorcising them out of people's lives and bringing healing, was he just contending with mythological creatures or embodied metaphors for mental illness? Or do we live in a demon-haunted world even now?

A Haunted Dorm Room

As a person who doesn't believe in ghosts, I was an odd choice for someone to perform an exorcism. I was in college, back when my wife and I were dating. She came to my room and woke me up early one morning. She was terrified, and wouldn't go back to her own room. She had been frightened awake by the strong sense that someone was standing next to the bed and had leaned close to her and said her name. That was pretty creepy… Even creepier, her roommate also heard the voice, whatever it was.

DOUG

I said I would do something about it because she was upset, and because I didn't want her to have to sleep in the lounge because she refused to return to her room and sleep there. So I thought about it for a bit, read through the Episcopalian exorcism rite on the Internet, then grabbed a Bible and my friend Adam and went to her room. I felt both silly and a little nervous—much like the feeling of entering a haunted house as an adult. I talked out loud to the ghost, or whatever it was, and told it something like, "You don't have to go home, but you can't stay here." I read some psalms and tried hard to think vibrant, lively, brightly lit thoughts while walking around the room. My friend Adam did something at the doorway with black candle wax and Kosher sea salt. That was that. No more voices, for whatever reason.

The point is, when faced with something another person believed to be an evil supernatural power, I felt pretty useless. As a young postmodern Protestant, I did not have anything in my toolbox for this kind of thing.

A Demon Named Legion[4]

Jesus had some tools in his toolbox for dealing with an evil supernatural power. In the Gospel according to Mark, Jesus and his

---

4. This section deals with Mark 4:35—5:20 (NIV).

disciples are crossing the sea of Galilee when a storm comes up that nearly capsizes the boat. The rabbi from Nazareth whispers, "Quiet! Be still!" and the raging wind and heaving sea, symbols of primordial chaos, die down and become completely calm. The terrified disciples are looking at each other and they say to each other, "Who is this guy? Even the wind and the waves obey him!"

Immediately as Jesus is stepping out of the boat, a frantic demon-possessed man comes and throws himself on his knees in front of Jesus. Mark, who is normally short on detail, lavishes attention on this tortured individual. He lived in the cemetery, among the dead. He screamed and cut himself with stones. He terrified the people in the area because they tried to bind him with ropes and even with chains, but with supernatural strength he tore the chains apart and broke the irons off of his feet. This is the guy upon whom many demon-possessions are based in the movies. He runs up toward Jesus and the disciples as they are climbing out of the boat. He has never met any of them before, but perhaps he has just witnessed the cessation of the storm, because he falls in front of Jesus and answers the question about Jesus' identity the disciples were asking earlier. "Jesus, Son of the Most High God," he says, "what do you want with me?"

This demon, like other demons, recognizes Jesus' true identity, because he, like the others, knows his Lord. To understand this we have to realize that the demonology of the ancient Near East is not the dualistic demonology of medieval Roman Catholicism. A "*daemon*" is just a spirit sent by the gods, or, in the case of first century Judaism, by Yahweh. There were many types of demons, but they were all intended by God to serve humanity. The key sign of disorder in an unclean spirit is that it has dominated, or "possessed," a person rather than giving that person life. In the Jewish worldview there are many "powers and principalities" in the world, all of them instituted by God, but many of them had become deeply sick. When a power designed to serve humanity begins to dominate and oppress humans, God does not mess around. God's judgment is harsh and final.

The demon, knees in the mud, begs Jesus not to torture him, which is ironic since the demon has been tormenting this possessed man. Then, realizing there is no way to avoid the impending judgment, he asks to be released into a nearby herd of pigs. Jesus assents and the demon-infested herd runs headlong off a cliff to a watery death in the lake below.

This episode is intensely symbolic. Fresh from pacifying the cosmic forces of chaos on the Sea of Galilee, Mark thrusts Jesus into direct conflict with an even more terrifying enemy: Rome. The demon addresses Jesus as, "Son of the Most High God," which includes the distinctive way that the Romans referred to the God of the Jews. Jesus then asks the demon his name (the only time he does this in the gospels), to which the demon replies, "Legion, for we are many." It so happens that, at the time, the Roman legion stationed in Judaea, which eventually took part in the destruction of the temple in 70 C.E., frequently used as their emblem the symbol of a boar.[5] The plunge into the lake of the pig-legion recalls the drowning of Pharaoh's army in the Red Sea.[6] The Gerasene demoniac, like Judaea itself, is occupied territory, and Jesus is driving the occupiers out.

Postmodern Demonology

We are all in occupied territory. Demons surround us and determine a great deal of our lives. All we have to do is point to the disproportionate number of minorities in prison;[7] to massive bank bailouts and massive CEO bonuses;[8] to environmental destruction and the loss of beauty;[9] to one in five children in the U.S. going to bed hungry;[10] to tens of thousands of people dying of starvation every day worldwide;[11] to epidemics of curable diseases among the poor;[12]

---

5. The Legion "X Fretensis" based in Judaea and Syria often used the boar as their emblem and was not only one of four legions responsible for the destruction of Herod's temple, but also led the siege of Masada, and later put down Bar Kokhba's revolt. The people of Judaea were oppressed by the boar for quite a while (http://en.wikipedia.org/wiki/Legio_X_Fretensis).

6. Exodus 14:21–31.

7. To understand the inherent racism of our prison system, read Michelle Alexander, *The New Jim Crow: Mass Incarceration in the Age of Colorblindness* (New York: The New Press, 2012).

8. The U.S. government has so far spent more than 600 billion dollars in bailout money, depending how you track these things (http://projects.propublica.org/bailout/). In the wake of the bailout, bonuses at the firms that received help went up by 17 percent (http://www.nypost.com/p/news/local/thanks_for_the_bailout_wall_street_wBruzG0E4x7ZJYcN0Nn9dL).

9. As many as 140,000 species currently become extinct each year, hundreds of times more than at any other time in human history: http://en.wikipedia.org/wiki/Biodiversity#Species_loss_rates.

10. According the the USDA, almost 17 million children in the U.S. are in food-insecure households (http://feedingamerica.org/hunger-in-america/hunger-facts/child-hunger-facts.aspx).

11. According to the United Nations' World Food Program, about 20,000 people die of hunger per day (https://www.wfp.org/hunger/stats). It is the world's number one health risk.

12. Dysentery alone kills more than 2 million people per year by conservative estimates (http://www.who.int/vaccine_research/diseases/diarrhoeal/en/index.html). It is easily preventable with clean water, and treatable with antibiotics.

to a thousand other horrors of the modern world, and we can trace it all right back to demons.

Demonic powers are not pointy-horned, trident-wielding monsters; they aren't even evil spirits that take over people's bodies and make their heads rotate 360 degrees. Demonic powers are the powers and principalities of this world when their collective spirituality becomes corrupted and they turn away from the common good—in other words, when they cease to serve humanity as God intended and instead dominate and oppress us.

The powers and principalities are groups of human beings who use resources and authority for the common good. Governments, businesses, civic organizations, NGOs, trade unions, and so on all have a purpose ordained by God—fostering justice and the flourishing of all people. Over time, however, many of these powers and principalities turn toward idolatrous purposes. They exist for themselves, seeking to perpetuate and swell their own power and control. They work to enrich their members rather than all of humanity. They use their power to dominate others rather than liberate them. They become demonic. Walter Wink calls these demonic powers and principalities the "Domination System" and describes them this way:

This overarching global economy and world political system, this overarching network of Powers is what we are calling the Domination System. It is characterized by unjust economic relations, oppressive political relations, biased race relations, patriarchal gender relations, hierarchical power relations, and the use of violence to maintain them all.[13]

The proper response to demonic possession is exorcism. You don't make friends with a demon. You cast it out. Those who have been dominated don't need to sympathize with their oppressor, they need liberty. The practice of expelling demons is about judging the fallen powers for what they are and extricating yourself from their influence.

We are so deeply locked in and bought into the Domination System that we don't see it. We're fish, and demonic enslavement is our water. It's everywhere, in everything, and so we are blind to it. It is possible, however, to learn to discern. Through participating in the story of God, we see another way—a way of life that is outside the

---

13. Walter Wink, *The Powers That Be* (New York: Doubleday, 1998), 39.

demonic powers that determine and destroy so much of human life. We learn that the way the world is is not the only way it could be.

In Jesus, we encounter someone who does things that would not occur to us to do. He casts out demons. But Jesus' most important exorcism wasn't supernatural at all. In the eleventh chapter of the Gospel according to Mark, Jesus "drives out" the money changers and dove sellers from the temple court.[14] They have become a demonic power, turned from their purpose of service toward domination and exploitation of the poor and vulnerable. Jesus cleanses the temple institution, exorcising the demon of greed from the heart of his society.[15]

When we understand the nature of demonic power, when we see that power in the systems that starve children, rape men and women, and abandon the old and the weak, it is time for some judgment, time for some discernment, time to tell the truth. We do this as Jesus did—disarmed. The only weapon we have is knowing our enemy's name, knowing all too well that it is our own name.[16]

As in Jesus' day, the demonic powers of our present darkness are everywhere—in the corrupt institutions that determine so much of our lives and care so little for our welfare. As in Jesus' day, they recognize their enemy when they see Him. When the body of Christ speaks prophetically against the Domination System, that system strikes back with the weapons of repression: humiliation, imprisonment, violence, and death. The whole Domination System works in concert to protect itself, mobilizing political contributions, television pundits, talk radio hosts, and the legal system where social order holds—and rape, death squads, and torture where society has broken down.

Perhaps the most demonic aspect of this system is that the people who participate in it may believe they are doing what is right. Their conscience and will have been subverted by the demonic power of idolatry as thoroughly as a raving maniac chained among the rocks in Jesus' day. They think that economic growth will save us; the police will save us; the next election will save us. In living this way, we bruise

---

14. Mark 11:15–19.

15. We take this insight from Ched Myers in his commentary on the Gospel of Mark: *Binding the Strong Man* (Maryknoll, N.Y.: Orbis Books, 2008). He argues that Jesus' cleansing of the temple is an exorcism. Specifically, he points out three specific verbal parallels between the eleventh chapter and Jesus' prophecy about "binding the strong man" in the third chapter.

16. Consider Doug's aside, *The Wizard of Earthsea* (spoiler alert), from "Love!"

ourselves on stones. Our world is no less demon-haunted than the world in which Jesus walked. The fact that our demons have anthems and logos and slogans and lobbyists doesn't make them any different.

The Bondage of the Will (Free Will Isn't)

Everyone reading this book is a participant in the demonic power of the Domination System, as well as a victim of it. We may understand this in the light of the scriptural witness about the powers and principalities of our world, but the demonic does not merely reside in human systems and structures. It resides in each of us, manifesting as the power to subvert our own will and freedom, to choose bondage for ourselves in the form of addiction.

Information-age society is defined by addiction. Who but a total junkie could ever wear clothing made by child slaves and people working in sweatshops for pennies an hour? What kind of addiction does it take to make us complacent in a society that systematically abandons the poor and mobilizes to defend the privilege of the rich?

Crackheads buy crack, again and again, even though the highs never lasts, even though each time they feels a little worse than the time before, even though it destroys their lives and their families and ultimately costs them everything. Our country invests hope and faith and money in Wall Street again and again, even though every time the bubble and the inevitable bust are a little worse than before, even though our hard-driving economy destroys lives and families, even though consumerism is burying us in garbage and pollution, and will ultimately cost us everything, as unsustainable economic practices come to a head sometime in the future.

Only addicts behave this way. Only addicts lie to themselves as doggedly and creatively as we do. Only addicts keep doing the same stupid thing over and over, even though any child could explain how it will destroy our lives in the end. It isn't a matter of explaining things. Explain how crack use looks from the outside to a crackhead and see how far that gets you. From inside the addiction, it makes a hideous kind of sense. It seems inevitable, inescapable. A doomed life. A room with no exits. The only way to be.

Left to our own devices, we choose the quick fix rather than the wiser path. This is what it looks like to be a part of Legion, one of many, all caught up in societal addiction. It looks like modern affluent consumer society. It looks like our supermarkets and our living rooms. It looks like what we call "culture."

What happens on the large scale continues on the small scale as well, in the forms of addiction with which we are more familiar. In a society defined by addictive behavior, it is no surprise that individuals fall into destructive patterns around alcohol, drugs, food, and consumption; no surprise that twelve-step meetings are full, and ubiquitous—and, for every person working the steps, there are probably a hundred more who should be.

It's easy to focus blame on the individual level—this enables us to divide society into the few who are addicts and the rest of us who are regular folks. It lets us avoid the fact that our way of life is founded on addiction. From top to bottom, from the individual scale to the grand scale of international economics, it's all our addiction.

Methadone

NICK

One day while I was making my chaplain rounds, I reached my very last new patient of the day. I looked down at my census, took a deep breath, memorized his name, knocked on the door and entered. The room was dark, the curtains drawn, the sixty-five-year-old patient was laying on the bed with his back turned to me.

He was a short, balding man of faith, one who was grateful for every day he had to read his Bible, and he was also an addict. He was a man who gave everything up for his addiction. I sat down and listened to his story of regret, his story of addiction in which he allowed himself to chose a high over his children, a relationship with a pipe over one with his wife. He sat with me, perched on the end of his bed, looking at me through worn eyes, broken teeth, and told me story after story about the horrors of his addiction and where it led him, waking up in filthy places not knowing how he got there, or what day it was.

My heart sank with each new story, with each broken relationship. He told me about his housing, living in a motel in the rundown section of town. He told me about living on his small disability checks, struggling to afford groceries, let alone enjoy life. But what really pushed me over the edge was when he told me about his only sense of community. It came through telling stories about his highs to his motel-mates, bonding over their addictions. While with them he would talk about his addiction as if the next high was his heart's desire, as if his addiction was not something that had taken everything from him. He felt the need to trade stories that glorified the very thing that afflicted him. He told me about how he felt like the only people that he could connect with in his life only appreciated him for his addiction.

His life was one so thoroughly lost to addiction that the addiction itself had become the center of identity and meaning for him—a void in his heart, annihilating the very thing which could have motivated him to reach for freedom.

Taking Out the Trash

The demons that addict, enslave, and oppress us don't come from hell. Hell is where they need to be sent.

Jesus never mentions hell in the gospels, but he does talk a lot about taking out the garbage. One of the words commonly (mis-) translated as "hell" in the gospel texts is Gehenna (*ge-hinnom*), which refers to a literal place—the smoldering garbage pit in the Valley of the Son of Hinnom outside of Jerusalem, where there is burning night and day, the gnashing teeth of scavengers, and where the "worm dieth not."[17] If you lived in or near Jerusalem, it was the worst place you could imagine. The smoldering refuse, the stench, the wild dogs digging around, the maggots—it was as bad as it gets. Gehenna was the place where the people tossed useless, repugnant things in order to get rid of them.

This burning garbage pit shows up a lot, especially in the Gospel of Matthew.[18] None of these instances refer to a place of eternal torment, with devils poking your butt with hot tridents to the soundtrack of Muzak versions of Ace of Base, or whatever "hell" would be. It's the city dump, and Jesus seems to be using it as a vivid, accessible image that his audience could easily understand. In brief, what gets consigned to the smoldering trash heap of Gehenna? All of the behaviors, authorities, systems, and powers that oppose the kingdom of God, because the kingdom is God's only purpose in the world, and when we find something for which there is no purpose, we throw it away.

---

17. In the ninth chapter of Mark Jesus quotes Isaiah 66:24, referring to a battlefield where the corpses of those who opposed God will be piled up in such a huge pile that the worms eating them will have enough food to live indefinitely and the fire to burn the pile will burn for a long time (but not forever).

18. Matthew 5:22, 29–30; Matthew 10:28; Matthew 18:9; Matthew: 23:15, 33; Mark 9:43, 45, 47; Luke 12:5.

It is not too much to say that we in the post-industrial West live in a throw-away culture. Through practices such as planned obsolescence and the focus on cheap goods made by the modern equivalent of slave labor in the global South and sold in ubiquitous big-box stores heaped with consumer goods for us to gather up and take home, the main thing that our culture currently produces is not scientific breakthroughs or new inventions or music or art—it is garbage.[19]

For each of us reading this book, it is easy to imagine that we could do with less clutter in our lives. We have too many things; we are buried in things: useless, temporary things that will never make us happy. Almost all of the things in our lives will ultimately be thrown away, ending up in some landfill or floating around in the oceans. We will replace them with yet more things, continuing the cycle of consumption until we die. We should all understand that we can easily make do with much less.

We ought to be willing to go farther than that, however. What we really need to throw away is the idea that life is measured by the accumulation of objects. We will never experience a fulfilling life if we spend our days in pursuit of possessions. We should take that idolatry, that act of putting something else in the place of God in our lives, and throw that idolatry onto the flaming garbage heap. We know that our possessions will not last, and should stop behaving as if they will.

As we grow away from our idolatrous lifestyle of destructive consumption, our view can expand a great deal. What we do on the personal scale, God has done on the cosmic scale. God is putting an end to the Domination System: the system of oppression, violence, and using people as a means to an end that currently governs so much of our lives. This way of life is no different from any other heap of garbage. Domination has no place in the kingdom. God has dealt the decisive death blow to the system, and what we experience are its death throes—wild, destructive, seemingly overwhelming, but limited, doomed, the last shuddering of a dying corpse; the flaring light of so much garbage, destined for incineration, as it rolls down into Gehenna.

---

19. The amount of garbage Americans produce in a given year is hard to estimate, but the EPA estimates it is around 1.35 billion pounds every day (http://curiosity.discovery.com/question/america-produce-trash).

In the bright dawning of this new day, we are invited to clean house. In light of this realization, we are required to live differently. To treat division through governments, races, genders, economic classes, and nationalities as if it is part of the kingdom is to engage in the foolish thinking and behavior of addicts—seeing that this view is empty, that it will only hurt us and not sustain us, and yet continuing to buy into it. With the death of the Domination System around us, and the death of the addictions among us and within us, we are set free like the Gerasene demoniac was set free: no longer chained among the dead.

Shit Rolls Downhill

ARIC

I was sitting on one of those long, uncomfortable benches they have outside courtrooms, shoulder to shoulder with a bunch of other people trying to avoid any eye contact lasting long enough to provoke the, "So, why are you here?" question. In my case, I was there to provide what comfort I could for a man guilty of intimate violence against his girlfriend. It was just a hearing to set a court date and extend the restraining order he was under, but it felt like I should attend, since all of the family attention and support was naturally (and correctly) going to the girlfriend.

He plead guilty, there being no other real option, and the hearing was quickly over.

Later, as we were walking out to my car (one of the consequences of his actions had been the suspension of his license), he began venting his anger—at the system, at his family, at his girlfriend, but mostly at himself. He ran through the usual litany of excuses for why he wasn't responsible for what he'd done: "I have bi-polar disorder, inherited from my alcoholic and abusive father, who divorced my mother when I was young and was replaced by a string of equally abusive boyfriends and step-fathers. I am under a lot of financial stress. I have heavy credit card debt and the recession led to cutbacks at work, meaning they shortened my hours, meaning they shrank my paycheck. The lack of funds means I can't afford my medication to stay emotionally stable, and to top it off my girlfriend loves to get in my face and provoke me."

Part of my support for him is helping him to sift through these excuses, to see them for what they are—aspects of his life that have shaped him, but do not control him—and to help him take responsibility for his actions. We do not do this by denying all of these painful experiences and circumstances. We do it by naming them, recognizing them, and then consigning them to the trash heap of mental baggage he will not permit to control him any longer. He has been the recipient of a lot of shit from forces bigger than him—his father, his genes, the economy—and so long as he inhabits that demon-haunted place all he can do is spread it around to people more vulnerable than himself. It all rolls downhill, and it keeps rolling until we have the courage to throw it in the fire; to say, "No more!"

The Lake of Fire and a Cosmic "No"

In the Revelation of John there is a lake of fire, a raging inferno of odorous brimstone, a metaphorical expansion of the trash heap at Gehenna, where God throws those things that are most opposed to the arrival of the kingdom. What is tossed in the fire experiences the "second death"—a permanent end. Everything that despises God is annihilated. Chief among the victims of these flames is the devil. Shortly thereafter, Death and Hades follow suit and are destroyed.[20]

Though this sounds like an image of horrific judgment to many contemporary Christians, in truth it is merely the flip side of the most hopeful vision in the New Testament. God is coming at last to dwell among the people, which means that every tear will be wiped from our eyes. There will be no more death, or mourning, or crying, or pain.[21] It is an extravagant hope that most of us easily dismiss as too good to be true, but to the writer of Revelation it is not unrealistic. He knows that for this vision to have any chance of becoming reality the old order of things has to pass away. There are many things to which God, and we, must say "No!" before God's "Yes!" to creation can be realized.

There are demons in our lives that need to be cast into the fire. They may clothe themselves in the structures and systems in which we are invested, and which are supposedly there for our well being, but whose collective spirituality has turned from service to domination. They may manifest as addictions, whether of the personal and chemical species, or the more insidious social and cultural variety. They may erupt in cycles of abuse and broken relationships that entrap us and keep us repeating the same destructive habits over generations. The demonic is an obstacle to our peace. It is garbage that piles up in our

---

20. Revelation 19:20; 20:10, 14–15; 21:8.
21. Revelation 21:4.

souls and prevents us from living into God's reality, garbage that needs to be thrown out.

In fact, we hereby reach through the pages of this book and declare in the name of Jesus Christ and by the power of the Holy Spirit that you are set free from the unclean spirit of Consumption, which whispers to you that you need more things in order to be complete, and helps cover your ears and turn your eyes away from the suffering that your wasteful lifestyle causes other human beings.

We cast out the demon Patriotism, which has lied to you and convinced you that the place where you happened to be born is especially favored by God, and the people there are more important than people born elsewhere.

We consign the demon Domination, which teaches that men must dominate women and the rich must dominate the poor and the violent must dominate the peaceful, to the burning trash heap.

We upend the unclean spirit of Economy, teaching that wealth must trickle down from the top, and that only the poor should suffer for their mistakes. This unclean spirit is hereby overturned, its hold shattered, its wealth scattered, its voice silenced.

We banish the unclean spirit Legion, which lives still, and goes by many names, and has convinced the whole world that security and safety are ours to grasp through the mechanism of war, and drives us continually to chain our brothers and sisters among the dead.

Further, we call on you to go out and expel the unclean spirits from the lives of those around you. Liberate yourselves and others from bondage to addictions, and relationships, and structures that oppress and control. Live lives unchained and free of the weight of garbage that serves no good end.

What God has expelled we must not hold onto, but we must join God in consigning it to the flames, even if that means giving parts of ourselves to the fire. As Jesus says, if your hand causes you to stumble cut it off, and if your eye causes you to stumble pluck it out. Jesus lets us know that none of us will get out unscathed. All of us will be "salted with fire."[22]

About that fire—the devil and Death and Hades and everything that causes suffering and pain is thrown into the fire and tormented for

---

22. Mark 9:43–49.

eternity, right? Not at all. The word translated "torment" (*basanizo*) in Greek has the primary definition of "testing a metal by a touchstone." A touchstone is a small tablet of dark stone, such as slate, with a finely grained surface. When you scrape soft metals such as gold against a touchstone, they leave a trace and you can tell by the color of the streak how pure or impure they are. The fire, in other words, is destroying the impurities, leaving behind only that which is fit to enjoy God's kingdom. This fire has a purpose—and an end. The kingdom is eternal, and nothing else is.

There is a power to cleanse even the most unclean spirit, and to heal even the deepest injury. God's cosmic "No!" of judgment and expelling contains within it a louder "Yes!" of reconciliation, freedom, and justice. When every demon and unclean spirit of fear, selfishness, violence, and domination is thrown out and consigned to burn up in the fire, we are purified and free at last.

***

The exorcist walked through Cynthia's home room by room, opening every cupboard and drawer, sifting through stacks of papers, and pulling out dusty boxes from closets to examine their contents, comparing each item against arcane lists. Every now and then he would spot something, and nod his head with secret knowledge. These objects would get thrown on the pile building on her front lawn, a random hodge-podge of her former possessions: clothes made in sweatshops, food traded unjustly, electronics containing materials mined in conflict zones, letters from her abusive ex-boyfriend and her over-sized clothes from two years ago. The exorcism took hours, purging her home of anything the exorcist deemed dangerous to her spiritual freedom. At the end of it the exorcist encouraged her to be strong and not to let the demons back into her home. She watched the truck filled with those former possessions drive away and went back inside to begin the work of living a new life.

Experiments in Expelling

■ Set aside a box, the size of a moving box. Over the course of a week or so, put things into that box that you don't really need or use anymore—clothes that don't fit, the spare blender, books you aren't going to re-read even if they might look impressive on your shelves. When the box is full, bring it down to alocal charity and donate it.

(Unless the stuff is garbage or broken, in which case, why is it in your home in the first place?) Then set out the box again, and repeat the process.

■ We eat a lot of disgusting things that are harmful to us—pick something and eradicate it from your diet. It could be red meat, processed sugar, caffeine, saturated fat, artificial sweeteners. This is not a diet—this is an exorcism.

■ Take an inventory of your life right now, and look to see whether there is anything that you are holding onto that might be harmful. Maybe you are holding a grudge, or you have a collection of rejection letters. Take the items associated with this toxic thing in your life, and find a place where it is safe to light a fire. Burn them. Douse the ashes and walk away.

■ Some of you reading this are struggling with serious addictions. It's time for you to seek treatment. It will probably be the most difficult thing you have ever done, but there are millions of people who have done it before you, and millions who will do it after. This is not an experiment—this is taking your life back. If you can turn to face your addiction and start working to overcome it, you are our personal hero. But who cares about what we think? You can be your own hero.

Heal!

The singing and shouting under the revival tent can be heard a mile away on the other side of town. Person after person comes down the center aisle for spiritual healing and delivery from demonic possession. A woman's rheumatoid arthritis fades and she dances a little jig. A young demon-haunted man finds clarity and shouts for joy. Claire is sitting in the second row in her wheelchair—no one meets her eyes, and she never comes down the aisle, knowing from hard experience that there's no point. Her faith isn't strong enough. She can't be healed.

Un-Well, Un-Male, and Un-Able

We'd like to introduce you to someone you've known all your life: the *default human being*. The default human being is the "base model," the image that most likely pops into your head when you read the word "human being"—or pops into the majority of heads in your culture. To be sure, this is entirely a cultural construct, and a problematic one at that, but it shapes the assumptions we make when we talk about health and healing. If you are living in the United States, then the default human being is, among other things, most likely a straight white male.

When we talk about health, we are talking about comparison. Everyone gets sick, and everyone's abilities diminish with age, and everyone dies. There is no recipe to avoid these things entirely, but we can compare them. How often do people get sick? How long do they remain able to be physically and mentally active? How old are they when they die, and what causes their deaths? Take body weight and composition as an example. If we say that being "obese"[1] is unhealthy, we are also saying that the healthy human being is thin. This is in contrast to other cultures in the world, in which what we call obese might be considered healthy and desirable, or Western culture at different times in history, when "healthy" meant something different entirely.

We can expand this idea of the default human being with regard to health—the default human being is a tall, relatively thin white male who remains active into his 70s. We could go on and on—he is only slightly bald at most, only has body hair in particular places, gets sick about once a year, has sex about once a week, etc. The point is, when we talk about health, we are talking about who our culture tells us we are supposed to be, as people.

This principle rears its ugly head in the context of sexism all the time. Too often, a woman is basically defined as a not-man, and this has been the case for thousands of years. To the sexist eye, women are simply deficient men who can also gestate babies (that is, they lack the male capacity for relatively consequence-free sex). This kind of sexist thinking is still widespread, but is being progressively challenged, and rightly so.

A similar principle is visible in conversations about disability—in fact, the distinction is in the name: *dis-ability.* A disabled person is defined by the their lack of a capacity that we attribute to the default human being we have in our minds. A dis-abled person gets a special bus, a special parking space, a special school, and Special Olympics (or Paralympics).

All of these ideas apply to any conversation about healing, because when we talk about healing, even in the church where we should know better, we are normally talking about restoring someone to the image of the default human being. We have a specific standard in mind, derived from our culture far more than from theology or the Bible or Jesus, and healing is restoring a person to a state that is closer to that standard.

Not only is this wrong, it is profoundly disappointing. Faith healers crisscross the country, or perform on television or the Internet,

---

1. Here we encounter our own cultural conditioning around health. Medically speaking, obesity correlates to a reduced life expectancy. At the same time, prioritizing life expectancy is part of our cultural definition of health.

but their abilities always seem quite limited when faced with people who are far from our cultural norm. Put another way, if a faith healer anywhere was regularly healing people of paraplegia, we all would have heard of this person, and the wheelchair industry would go bankrupt once the trick became common knowledge. Apart from anecdotal evidence and the occasional healing story that is scientifically indistinguishable from happy coincidence, we just don't see dramatic supernatural healing—certainly nowhere in the Western world, and nowhere else in the world where they have video cameras and doctors to verify results.

This leaves us with two possible conclusions. One is that God does not heal anyone apart from medicine, which requires no particular faith in God or even personal virtue to work. This is a reasonable conclusion. Given the vast distance between common claims about God's healing and the actual healing we see in the world we all inhabit, it looks like God is just not in the healing game.

The other option is that we have it wrong—that we incorrectly assume that healing is bringing a person closer to our cultural norms.[2] In that case, healing wouldn't just mean making a person more like what our culture says that person should be. It would mean something *better*. Sick people are not merely failing to be healthy; women are not merely defective men; disabled people are not lesser people.

Why Hasn't My Faith Healed Me?

ARIC

For five years now I've been visiting Laura at least once a month. She is mostly confined to her bed with a series of health issues that began with a car accident over thirty years ago. On good days her pain is bearable, and she can smile and tell you stories about her sons in the military, and her grandchildren who she rarely sees because they live far away. The good days are rare, though, and on more than a few occasions I have sat with her while she told me that she was contemplating suicide because she could see no end to her suffering.

Laura believes fervently in miraculous healing. She reads the stories of Jesus' and the disciples' healing miracles in the New Testament, and whispers the phrase Jesus often employed, "Your faith has made you

---

2. For an impassioned sermon on this, see Nadia Bolz Weber's "Sometimes It Hurts," http://www.patheos.com/blogs/nadiabolzweber/2012/09/sometimes-it-hurts-a-sermon-on-healing/

well!" to herself. She continually seeks spiritual comfort from a variety of sources. I am not the only minister she asks to visit her regularly. She has had healing ceremonies, anointing with oil, laying-on-of-hands, reiki, acupressure, and everything else tried on her in addition to the medical care she receives. None of it has relieved her agony.

Laura's belief in supernatural healing is not helping her. It is crushing her. She alternates between blaming herself, believing that she is simply not faithful enough to merit the healing she needs, and blaming God— believing that God must be punishing her with this excruciating existence. The churches that continue to feed this belief by promising God will restore her to our cultural ideal of wholeness only heighten her dilemma. With so many faithful people putting a word in for her with the big guy upstairs, how could her body remain in such a broken state?

Meanwhile, Laura's decades-long pursuit of supernatural aid troubles those Christians who, like her, believe in healing miracles, but can't offer better explanations for this woman's anguish than, "God works in mysterious ways." Rather than ask whether there is a better way to understand health and healing, they turn away from Laura, finding it easier to ignore the situation than change their beliefs.

We Do Not Have Souls

Many of us were taught that the soul is a disembodied, noncorporeal essence that inhabits your body and then leaves it behind when your body dies. The soul, thus freed, moves on to the afterlife, or whatever comes next. This is a very popular view, but it has nothing whatsoever to do with the Bible, Judaism, or early Christianity.

There is no word in the Bible that is rightly translated as a disembodied essence that detaches upon death and floats away. The closest to this are the various words that are usually translated as "spirit," sometimes as "breath," which refer to God's power to give life, or God's presence, or the presence of one of the "powers and principalities."[3]

The many words that are translated as "soul" in English have other meanings, such as "life," "living being," or "heart," or "mind," or "self." The soul is not at all disembodied, or separate from bodily

---

3. We talk about "powers and principalities" in a lot more detail in "Expel!"

existence, at least not in the view of the many different people who contributed to the Bible.[4] Rather, it is a life-heart-mind-self. The most common Greek word in the New Testament translated as "soul" is *psuche*, the word from which we get "psyche." In English, psyche refers to the totality of a person's consciousness: their experiences, thoughts, feelings, emotions, memories, hopes, and so on. Everything that we experience is part of our psyche.

Psuche was used as a Greek translation of the Hebrew word *nephesh* in the Old Testament. Nephesh refers to something like a "living being," and when psuche shows up in the New Testament, it is a good guess that the meaning is intended to be more like "living being," rather than the disembodied ideal that we later borrowed from Greek philosophy.[5]

In talking about healing, the soul means the whole. Your soul is all of you, all together, interconnected in infinite ways. It is your *psuche*, your *nephesh*, your self. For healing to matter, it must take into account our soul, our totality. Healing can't just act on one part of a person as if that part was not connected to all of the other parts. We can't help someone to wholeness by treating only physical symptoms. Nor can true health refer to something nonphysical—if a person's soul is healed, their body will be just as involved as their mind.

What we mean by a soul, a whole person, is not just a substitute for that default human being. Being whole is not the same as living up to societal ideals. What this means is that a person with an illness may be just as whole as a person our society defines as healthy. A woman is a whole person, just as a man is. A person we see as disabled is not necessarily any less whole than a person who has more physical capabilities. If we are to abandon our assumptions about what a "whole" person would look like, we still need some idea of wholeness that comes from outside our culturally constructed notions of gender, health, ability, and so on.

---

4. We draw this idea of the "soul" from many sources, but a good place to get an overview is the *Harper Collins Bible Dictionary, Revised Edition*, pg. 1055: "Soul." The dualism we normally associate with the word was, according to Harper Collins, introduced with the Wisdom of Solomon.

5. Wikipedia tells us that Plato, in his dialogue Phaedo, introduces the idea of ideal Forms, perfected objects compared to which physical objects are like a wavering shadow cast on a cave wall. So, with Wikipedia, we will blame Plato.

For Christians, that vision of wholeness is Jesus Christ. We are so accustomed to having Jesus lifted up as the answer that you probably saw this coming, but consider what it means—our icon of wholeness is a criminal, betrayed by the religious leaders of the day, tortured and executed by the state, and wounded in ways that even Resurrection does not cure.

Running Around the Baptistry

NICK

When I began serving in Columbia, Missouri, our church discovered something: despite the fact that there are churches on nearly every corner (with some exceeding the 5,000 member mark) there was a total lack of spiritual care for the differently abled and their families in our city. Other services are plentiful, including therapists, aids, helpers, and a wonderful degree program at our university. In fact, some residents of our city moved here specifically to be near the services offered for their family members, but our churches were not similarly responsive.

People with disabilities and disabled members of their families told us that they feel totally unwelcome in our churches. Our church decided to do something about it, and formed a wonderful program we call "All God's Children," which seeks to offer a place in our community for families with children with disabilities. As we started the program, I got to meet the stream of families who jumped at the opportunity to participate in a church with offerings for their kids, and my heart broke hearing each story. I listened to them tell me about how unwelcoming every community of faith had been to them. Some were flat out asked to take their noisy, disruptive children and go. Some were gawked at or mocked when they entered the building. Some were told the church didn't have the time or energy to help them care for their family members. Most had one or two stories of faith communities that told them they were welcome but nothing ever changed to accommodate them, despite their inquiries for help and services.

My favorite moment to date for the program was watching our senior minister chase a young man with autism around the baptismal pool to sprinkle him with water (which was the plan since he was deathly afraid of being dunked). Suddenly this young man stopped, smiled, jumped for joy into the pool, and then paraded out of the baptismal waters along side his two sisters and their mother, with the minister still trailing behind and yelling something about the waters of life. This family became new members of our family of faith together.

My tradition, the Disciples of Christ, claims to be *"a movement of wholeness in a fragmented world."* Watching those our society calls fragmented demonstrate their wholeness in our community has made me consider what our claim means in a new light.

Broken, and Therefore Whole

Paul tells us that Jesus is "firstborn from among the dead"—the first one to be resurrected by God.[6] Jesus' Resurrection is the source of a Christian hope of resurrection. But when Jesus is resurrected, he is still wounded. So, either God got it wrong, and didn't resurrect Jesus thoroughly enough, or it is possible to be both whole and wounded. Let's assume that God got it right—that God's intent in resurrecting Jesus was to resurrect him as still wounded, still a criminal, still an outcast rejected by the religious authorities.

In talking about healing, about *restoration of wholeness,* which is the least that healing can possibly mean, we are not talking about healing a person's "soul" while leaving the body broken. We are not talking about restoring a person to a cultural ideal. We are not talking, necessarily, about sealing up every injury or driving out the things we define as illness. In order to restore our cultural definitions of things such as health, or mental health, or capability, we use the technologies that our culture provides: medicine, psychotherapy, prosthetic limbs. It is still often a beautiful thing to be restored in these ways—cultural ideals can still have value, even if they don't come from God. The problem is that we also seek to "restore" people through other aspects of our culture: shaming, abuse, marketing, oppression. It is beautiful when a child with hearing loss hears for the first time through a cochlear implant. It is disgusting when a man is told he is defective because he is not aggressive toward his wife. Our culture practices both forms of restoration.

How can we tell the difference between the kind of healing that brings greater wholeness and the kind of healing that is just reinforcing cultural biases and our concept of the default human being? One way is to have purpose in mind. It is impossible to

---

6. Colossians 1:18 (NIV).

understand how to heal a person if you do not know that person's purpose. When we use the cultural methods listed above to heal, they are all used for a purpose which our culture defines. We are restored to the capacity to be who we are told to be and to do what we are supposed to do. Women and men are restored to their gender roles. The sick are restored to our prevailing definition of health. Those we call disabled are restored to the abilities to which we assume every whole person should have access.

If we are interested in what God's purposes are, one of the first things we encounter is the fact that God's purposes are not like our purposes much of the time. While we are taught to accumulate possessions, God calls us to give them up.[7] When we are told to cling to life, God calls us to let go of our lives.[8] When we are trained to hate our enemies, God calls us to love them.[9] When we are given a script for "masculine" and "feminine" behavior, God declares that there is no longer male and female,[10] and lifts up "effeminate," nurturing men, and "masculine," assertive women: Deborah leads men in battle[11] and Jesus' disciples are urged to cuddle children.[12]

These purposes—giving up possessions, letting go of life, loving enemies, breaking gender stereotypes—require a different kind of healing, a different kind of restoration. It may be that a wounded, "broken" person would be *more* able to fulfill God's purposes, precisely for the same reasons that a culture would not find any use for that person. We see this in Jesus. Taking Jesus' Resurrection to be the ultimate expression of God's restoration, we see that Jesus is restored to life, but it is life of a different kind. He is resurrected to new life, but his wounds remain.

With the resurrected Christ as our model, it is possible to see healing not as restoration, but as a kind of disfigurement. To be good at giving away possessions is to be crippled in accumulating them; to be empowered to lose your life will come across as a severe liability; to love one's enemies is to fail to appear patriotic and brave, to be a

7. Luke 12:33; Matthew 19:21; Mark 10:21.
8. Matthew 10:39.
9. Matthew 5:43–44.
10. Galatians 3:28.
11. Judges 4—5.
12. Matthew 19:13–15.

defective competitor and citizen; to break gender roles is to be reviled as "queer," "bitch," "fag," "slut."

Perhaps it is impossible to be made whole by God and to also be "healed" by the usual standards. People who have been made whole by God will never again fit into the world as they once might have. Their purposes will no longer align with the purposes assigned to them due to their positions in society. They will be drawn in by God and cast out by others.

If God's healing ended there, it would be a bitter, lonely existence.

The Wounded Body

Wholeness and purpose do not happen in a vacuum—to be fully healed is to be reintegrated into community. The wounded are always outcasts. The sick, the disabled are set apart, taken out of their community and marked out as different, as less, as threatening liabilities. They receive "special" education and "special" parking spaces and a "special" kind of anonymity—ignored by most, and often subject to awkward politeness at best. A specific disability spills over into assumptions about all of a person's capacities.

This has been true throughout history. When Jesus healed people, he had to put special effort into making sure those people were then received into community. He had to tell them what to say to people when people asked what happened; he had to remind them to present themselves to the temple authorities so that they could be declared officially "clean." He would publicly touch them when no others would dare, leading by example, behaving as if the unclean were clean so that they might be accepted as such.[13]

To be healed is to be welcomed into full participation in community. This must include addressing the stigmas and outsider status that come along with woundedness, lack of certain abilities, minority status, nontraditional family type, and any number of other factors that our culture rejects as brokenness. To the degree that the wounded are cut off, those who are being healed must be brought in.

But if wholeness in the pattern of Christ is as counterintuitive as we say it is, then returning to our former communities may not be possible. If being whole means being oriented to God's purposes, then it will also require a community that is oriented to God's purposes. In

---

13. Matthew 8:1–4, and see our discussion of cleanliness in "Praise!"

order to heal, we may find ourselves having to depart communities that do not accept us, seeking new ones that embrace us, wounds and all. Paradoxically, it is being loved in our brokenness that opens the possibility of wholeness.

Not only is Christ raised with his wounds intact, but those wounds become the glue, the binding agent of the community that formed in his name. His disciples recognize him by his wounds. Many people are familiar with the story of Thomas who was appropriately skeptical of stories of Jesus' Resurrection until he saw the wounds in his master's side, but few notice that just a few verses before that incident the other disciples only realize who it is that just appeared in their midst when he displays his wounds.[14] In these appearances Jesus again and again says, "Peace be with you," and urges them to forgive sins, indicating that his purpose for visiting is reconciliation. He acts to forge a community predicated on the integrity of his own injured person.

The post-Resurrection vignette which really drives this home is Jesus' encounter with Peter on the beach in the Gospel according to John.[15] Jesus asks Peter three times, "Do you love me?" Each time Peter responds more emphatically that he does, but on the third time the text tells us that Peter's feelings are hurt. Why did this repetition bother Peter? Because Peter had denied his love for Christ three times when his teacher was on trial before the Sanhedrin. Recognizing the symmetry, Peter realizes that Jesus is offering him redemption. His guilt and the awareness of his forgiveness suddenly collide, and it hurts. Jesus instructs Peter to "feed his sheep"—in other words, to nourish the community that Jesus is creating. Jesus' wounds become the doorway to Peter's forgiveness. Peter's wound of guilt becomes the doorway to his faithful ministry.

This is what the church is intended to be: a community oriented to God's purposes where people are loved into wholeness. This is not accomplished by ignoring our wounds, excluding the wounded from our midst, or by communal repression. An invisible person who climbs out of his wheelchair but returns to invisibility is not healed.

---

14. John 20:19–29. More poetically, the disciples in Luke only recognize Jesus when he breaks the bread, which only a few days beforehand he had described as his body, broken for their benefit, and by which they should remember him (Luke 24:13–35).

15. John 21:15–19.

A social outcast whose disease is cured but who is still derided by her society is not healed. A person who is convinced or coerced into enacting an assigned gender role in order to be accepted is not healed. It is the person who is enabled, even encouraged, to live out his *or* her full, God-given purpose in community who is healed.

What Every Church Wishes It Was

DOUG

During an interview on Clyde Rohr's game-design podcast Theory From the Closet,[16] *Vincent Baker, a well-known indie game designer, said that the game design community that he had found*[17] *was "what every church wishes it was, but isn't." What he meant is that he had found, in other gamers and game designers and artists and writers, an organic community of people who cared about his creative projects, and who would put a lot of time and effort into making his dreams a reality.*

This has been my experience as well. Even though designing games is only a hobby for me, I have encountered literally hundreds of people who are willing to help me, even when all they know about me is that I am a gamer and I have some creative projects. In turn, I have had the chance to help others, occasionally for pay but mostly for trade or just for fun, with their own work. Something about engaging in a hard, creative process, all in the pursuit of adding more fun and more stories to the world, seems to draw people into community. In the context of that community, it is possible to find identity, to be valued and to be accepted despite differences. This is just one example of how people will seek out communities of meaning and inspiration, whether in church or, very often in my generation, outside of church.

The majority of gamers and game designers are, in my experience, either nonreligious or not very religious, but maybe they have found something better than religion: passion, and a community of like-minded people who will help them live out their passion, hold them to high standards, and provide support when things go wrong. These are all what religion should be about, but there are a lot of game designers out there who didn't experience these things in church, which is probably why they never came back.

16. Show 059: Interview with Vincent Baker.
17. The Forge: http://www.indie-rpgs.com/forge/index.php.

Fully God, Fully Human, Full Communion

God doesn't free people *from* things, God frees people *for* a purpose. The resurrected Christ didn't lose the wounds in his hands or in his side—he left blood-stained footprints and handprints wherever he went. He had open wounds that never closed. The resurrected Jesus is in part defined by his wounds. The marks of a crown of thorns are still on his head, and the slashes and welts left by the Centurion's lash remain on his back.

This is the image of God, the firstborn from the dead, both human and divine—a wounded God for a wounded people. The resurrected Christ embodies God's purpose fulfilled, and we can look to the resurrected Christ to see how it is that God heals. Christ is not transformed into who the Judeans or Romans in Jerusalem wanted him to be. He remains impoverished, an outsider, and a convicted criminal. Jesus' purpose, however, is fulfilled—he is the source of life, victorious over death, the embodiment of unkillable love. Furthermore, Christ is not raised alone—he is sent back in order to give birth to a new community, and it is this community, the Church, that draws upon his life and lives out his purposes for the world.

Christ heals his broken followers and refashions their community in the midst of fear and doubt, betrayal and abandonment. Participation in this community consists of the use of our passions, abilities, and wounds to serve those in need and to make the world better. Christ's followers go out to heal the world, to bind up wounds and to receive wounds in turn, to accept harm rather than inflict it, to seek reconciliation rather than retribution, to embrace rather than exclude. As we are healed, we are to offer healing to others. This means that we do not impose cultural norms on other people, but rather do what we can to support and empower them to live out their purpose. We do not turn anyone away, but rather reach out to the last and the least, the broken and the wounded, and welcome them into our shared life. In the midst of this community of broken people, social outcasts and deviants, we find ourselves and our purpose, together.

In a way, this shared life is the ultimate violation of cultural norms. Every culture has methods of labeling and defining and categorizing people as healthy or sick, clean or unclean, strong or weak, valuable or disposable, insider or outsider, safe or threatening. When we share our lives and purpose, all of these distinctions are removed, leaving only a community of radical equality that exists apart from whatever it is our culture tells us to be, whether it is Hellenistic culture in the Roman Empire, European culture in Christendom, or Evangelical Protestant culture in the United States. These divisions, this hierarchy, and these biases are what need to be healed.

We remain, after the healing, people who are fully human despite our brokenness, who share full communion despite our differences, walking in the footsteps of a God who is whole despite being wounded.[18]

***

Lawrence stood in front of the congregation along with his fellow ordinands, stating his vows with conviction, and accepting the blessing of the elders of the church. Just a few years ago this day would have been inconceivable. The words of rejection cast his way still rung in his ears. The pain of past wounds remained, but it was joy that now caused tears to run down his cheeks. Perhaps he would never be accepted by his former friends or even his own family, but these people embraced him and celebrated his gifts, and made him feel worthy of love. As they placed the stole on his shoulders, he committed his life to restoring others like himself to wholeness and dignity.

Experiments in Healing

▧ Pay attention to the media you consume in a given day. Note every way in which you differ from the "norm" with which you are presented. Strike up a conversation with someone who is different from you about what media they consume, and whether they've noticed some of the same things. Compare the people you see in mass media with the people all around you.

▧ Write down what you think your higher purpose might be for your life. Then, commit to doing one thing that is related to that purpose. Afterward, reflect: Do you feel more whole?

---

18. Hat tip to Henri Nouwen for the idea of the "Wounded Healer." We have picked up on his themes but taken them in some slightly different directions with our interest in communities of radical equality that transgress supposed distinctions between the wounded and the healthy.

■ Reflect on how you have been formed and nurtured by a community you are part of: your family, church, yoga class, gaming group, buddies from school you meet for drinks, whomever. Commit to saying something to them about what they have meant in your life.

■ Invite an outsider in. Find a new person in your apartment complex or neighborhood or office or school, someone who doesn't "fit in," and invite that person to something you do regularly with others— but not as a token; *really* invite this person.

Intercede!

The time of intercession comes, and there's a short silence before Marge gets up to speak. She asks God to help the soldiers overseas, and to bring them home safe. Next is Ed, who lifts up a local family that lost their house to flooding. After a bit Zack stands up in the back and asks God to help with school because he's nervous about finals. Last is Wendy, who asks everyone to think of her sister-in-law, who is in the hospital after a heart attack. The preacher stands up at the end and ties all of their concerns together into a shared expression, and speaks for those who were silent about their struggles. When the service is done, everyone feels a little better, hopes that God will help those people, and they go out for brunch, feeling more at peace.

Heroism Isn't Super

The contours of perfectly sculpted muscles: square jaws and cleft chins; fluttering capes and distress calls; leaping over buildings and into action against overwhelming odds; running toward the gunshots when everyone else is running away; emerging from the fire, unburned.

The elements of heroism made iconic by pulp novels, comics, and movies are embedded deep in our psyches. It takes a special kind of person to stand up on behalf of others, a special kind of person to face what others cringe from. It takes a hero to intercede. We love heroic stories so much that, over time, human beings with flaws, context, and shortcomings are transformed into heroes in our minds. George Washington was able to lie. Gandhi was not a model husband or father. Ronald Reagan sold arms to Iran to fund Contras in Nicaragua. Thomas Jefferson had illegitimate children with his slaves. Mother Teresa was a crafty business woman. Despite the facts, we dip our memories of certain people in bronze, and polish them to a high sheen. We remember them the way we want to remember them, not the way that they actually were. When someone intrudes with the facts of history, it can feel like a violation, like the moment we learned that Santa Claus was just Dad eating the cookies and drinking the milk that we left out the night before.

Grand acts of heroism, of self-sacrifice, inspire us, and cause us to lionize the people who do heroic things. They thrill us, and something inside of us moves in response to these stories. Yet in the very moment that we are moved, we also remember—*we* are just regular people. We are not heroes. We are not powerful or brilliant or courageous. We do not risk everything to do what is right.

The problem with imagining superheroes is that they lead us to assume that heroes are different. They are born different than the people around them, or their circumstances transform them by some alchemy from mundane into magnificent. They are primed for heroism in a way that we are not. Superman, an iconic American hero for decades, crash-lands in an Iowa cornfield, a visitor from a distant galaxy. A great hero, who represented "truth, justice, and the American way," was not American. He was an alien who flew in from the outside to rescue us.[1]

Church is rife with this kind of thinking. We have taken the innocuous little word *saint* and changed it from a term applied to all disciples into a title granted only to specific extraordinary individuals who not only demonstrated courage and conviction in their lives, but who are credited posthumously with interceding on behalf of the ordinary faithful like us. Interceding in situations of great peril or suffering is consequently projected into the realm of supernatural powers. Great men and women must reach into this life from beyond the veil to accomplish miraculous rescues.

Of course, the precedent for treating saints as exceptional individuals is well established in the way we portray Jesus. Despite

---

1. The contrast between the origin stories of Superman and Jesus of Nazareth is striking. Superman is an alien who came to earth to be a God among men, sharing none of our weaknesses. Jesus is a God who came to earth to be a servant and a slave, exemplifying all of our weaknesses. Intercession is not work for the invincible, but for the fragile.

ancient doctrinal insistence on the full humanity of Jesus of Nazareth, we are more comfortable with him as savior than as servant, or slave, or victim. Jesus commanded his disciples to do everything he was doing, and greater feats besides,[2] but we focus on his singular actions, his unique identity, and his sinless perfection. We dwell on his divinity, and this plays out in worship when we spend time hoping God will intervene and save us, or remembering when God intervened to save others in the past. We reduce the life of discipleship to the equivalent of staring up like baby birds, waiting to be fed. We forget that we are intended to fly.

And thus we have convinced ourselves that intercession is supernatural, and that heroes are different from the rest of us. It's reassuring to think of heroism as something that other people do—people who are not made the way we are made; people who do not have what we have to lose.

This false perception is reassuring because it allows us to ignore the endless opportunities for heroism that we have in our own lives. There are countless anecdotes, even sociological experiments,[3] that tell us about how hard we will work to avoid interceding, even when we risk nothing but inconvenience—the person lying in an alley calling for help while busy commuters walk past, studiously ignoring him; the unconscious person who is stepped over almost as a matter of course; the family with the broken-down car on the side of the road that waits for hours for anyone to pull over and offer help.

One of the ways we find to salve our consciences is to think to ourselves, "Surely someone else will help that poor person—I'm just too busy." The problem is that when everyone thinks that way, no one intercedes. What if everyone else who sees a person in need makes the same excuse? What if you are the only one who might actually do something to help that person? If you help, it might cost you five or ten minutes; maybe a phone call or a conversation. If you don't help, it costs you much more than that.

---

2. John 14:12.

3. John Darley and Daniel Batson published one of the most famous papers looking into helping behavior. The study was entitled From Jerusalem to Jericho: A study of situational and dispositional variables in helping behavior. It showed that even busy seminary students on their way to preach sermons on the Good Samaritan were likely to step over a person in distress in order not to be late to preach their sermon (http://experimentaltheology.blogspot.com/2011/06/from-jerusalem-to-jericho-on-hurry.html).

We hear the words now and then, in church perhaps, that tell us that the greatest love is to lay down our lives for another.[4] We think, "I'm not ready to die for someone—that's the kind of thing a hero might do, but not me." Fair enough. But consider this: Can you lay down your life, can you set your life aside, for a few minutes? This might be all it takes to make a difference in someone's life. You don't have to die for the first person you see who is in need—all you have to do, in order to intercede, is do *something*.

The Carnegie Hero Fund

DOUG

The fact that heroism is actually much more common than we might think first hit me when I was listening to Radio Lab one day. It was Season 9, Episode 1, an episode entitled "The Good Show."[5] The show was about "good": people doing good things, and why they do them, or in other cases fail to do them.

One of the guests on the show was a guy named Walter F. Rutkowski. He was representing something I'd never heard of before, called the Carnegie Hero Fund[6]. In brief, they search for stories of contemporary heroes, and they recognize those heroes and give them a small amount of money. To do this, they started with a definition of what a hero is. For them, a hero is someone who risks his or her own life on behalf of someone this person does not know personally. It has to be a serious risk, a serious chance of dying, and it can't be for the person's child or spouse or friend. It has to be for a stranger.

Okay—risking your life for a stranger—you would think that would be pretty rare. Even when soldiers risk their lives, it is for fellow soldiers— not strangers, but people who might be their best friends, and are at least comrades in arms. Firefighters risk their lives for strangers, but they do so alongside other firefighters, and they train for a couple of years to learn how to do that. These people the Hero Fund is looking for are just ordinary people, with no special training.

I think the most striking thing about the interview was Rutkowski talking about how, when they first started off, the problem that they had was that there were too many heroes. Too many people risking their lives

---

4. John 15:13
5. http://www.radiolab.org/2010/dec/14/
6. http://carnegiehero.org/awardees/

for strangers. They weren't able to recognize all of them, or they would have burned through their endowment in a very short time. They actually had to go back and make the definition of "hero" more stringent, so that they weren't overwhelmed with heroism.

This is not the problem I'd expect. What I imagine is a group of bored, sad people staring at phones that aren't ringing, tossing newspapers into the recycling bin with a sigh, realizing that there are no heroes out there. A victory for cynicism, and, in a sense, a way of letting myself off the hook.

But sometimes we surprise ourselves. I remember on a road trip with my wife, we were driving through a rainstorm, and we watched as, just a few cars in front of us, a big white SUV fish-tailed and then rolled entirely, bouncing off the guardrail and coming to a stop partially crumpled and upside-down. As we watched it tumble in seeming slow-motion, we could see a family being thrown around inside, a mother, father, and a child. Without thinking about it, we intervened, helping the family out of the wrecked vehicle, calling 911, and then keeping them calm until paramedics arrived. We didn't do anything extraordinary, but of the hundreds of cars that passed by the wreck, we were the ones who stopped.

Baby Steps

It's probably true that not everyone is able to do something worthy of the Carnegie Hero Fund. This is true, but it is a poor excuse. Sometimes intercession is hard, but most of the time, it's pretty simple. You won't pass a burning building every day with people in the third-story window shouting for help. You will almost certainly, however, come across someone in your daily life who needs help—probably before you finish reading this book.

To intervene is very simple. You can start off easy, get some momentum. Remember that your biggest hero was probably a lot more like you than you think. He or she had plenty of faults and failings and fears. This hero may have had skills you don't, but you have skills the hero didn't as well. You will certainly have opportunities this person did not have. The big difference is becoming an intercessor— deciding that you are not going to be the person who walks past, hoping someone else does the right thing. You are going to lay down your life, just for a little while, and make a difference in someone else's life.

If Only They Knew You

Ruth is sleeping under a bridge tonight because she doesn't know you. If she was your friend and you knew that she would be making her bed under a freeway overpass, you would do something. You would offer your couch for a couple of nights, or you would make a phone call to a relative with a cheap room for rent and offer to pay. You would intercede because you know Ruth, and you can't just let someone you know sleep under a bridge.

But Ruth doesn't know you, or anyone else with the resources to help her, so there she is.

Juan just finished his school lunch. It's Friday and it is the last meal he will eat for over forty-eight hours, because his family runs out of money toward the end of the month and they have to skip meals. If it weren't for the government assistance program that pays for Juan's lunch at school he would go hungry much more often. If you knew that this classmate and friend of your child was going hungry on Saturday night while you order pizza, you would be inviting him over for dinner. You would intercede.

But Juan's family doesn't know your family; English is not his first language; and you've never seen his parents at the school events, so Juan doesn't eat when the end of the month comes around.

Michael has been contemplating suicide for months. If you were friends with Michael you might have noticed the signs of depression. He might have confided in you, in which case you certainly would have done everything in your power to get him the help he needs, to assure him that he is worthy of love, and you would have refused to leave him alone. You would intercede because you know Michael, and you wouldn't abandon someone you know to despair.

But Michael doesn't know you, so he starts making a plan to end his life. He can only fall one step lower, and he's going to take that last step on his own terms.

The root of most human suffering is relational.[7] Think about the things that have really crushed you in your life—most of them probably had to do with a relationship with another person. What we're talking about here, though, is that people not only suffer because

---

7. Hugh Hollowell of Raleigh, North Carolina, really lives this concept. He is the founder of Love Wins Ministries (http://lovewins.info/), which is a ministry of pastoral care and presence for the homeless and at-risk population of that city. They strive to transform each others' lives not through programming but through relationship.

of some toxic relationships in their lives, they also suffer because they lack healthy, supportive relationships and the resources that come with them.

If you are educated enough to read this book and can afford to buy it, then you probably have friends and family who have some spare money. You may have even had to ask them for help now and then. You are more than one step away from homelessness—if you had to, you could move in with parents or friends or other family until you were past whatever trouble had come your way and could begin to recover. Because of the relationships you have, you have a kind of safety net that can catch you before you hit bottom. Or, you might serve as the safety net for your own friends and family, if you are more fortunate than they are.

It makes sense that if more people had more relationships, these nets would widen, and they would catch more people before they fell through, before they ended up sleeping under overpasses, or going hungry at the end of the month, or quietly planning their own deaths. The more people we know personally, and the more willing we are to help them, the wider that net becomes. It might even be possible for the net to be wide enough to catch everyone. We don't think, as followers of Jesus, that we should be satisfied with anything less.

In the past couple of decades, it might have been easier to think of desperate poverty as someone else's problem. The truth is, though, that nearly half of all Americans would struggle to come up with $2,000 within thirty days. This fact is important, because, for the National Bureau of Economic Research, $2,000 seemed like a reasonable amount of money that some significant mishap might cost you. That's a trip to the ER, or major repairs on the vehicle you use to get to work, or any number of things that might come up in a normal life. The total of $2,000 was chosen because it represents a decent emergency fund, or, in this case, the ability to come up with emergency funds when you really need to.[8]

This widespread financial vulnerability, in which fewer than half of U.S. households have any emergency funds, is only going to increase in the next few years. Record home-value depreciation, people having to default on debts they can no longer maintain, disappearing jobs

---

8. Read the full paper on financially fragile households from the National Bureau of Economic Research (http://www.nber.org/papers/w17072).

and falling wages in the jobs that do exist will continue to act together in order to make people more vulnerable than they were a decade ago.

There are, according to the National Bureau of Economic Research, as many as 150 million people in the U.S. who are one emergency away from serious trouble. They have no safety net at all. They, like an increasing number of people, may find themselves suddenly caught in a downward spiral. For some, that downward spiral will lead under a bridge, or to persistent hunger, or even to the morgue.

Now, consider this: If each of the people who had an emergency fund knew one of the people who did not have one, that number would drop from 150 million to zero. This is not through better government policies or more personal responsibility, but through more, and more loving, relationships.

Many will be thinking, "Shouldn't someone else bail them out, rather than make us help each other? Isn't that why I pay taxes?" If we're honest, some people are just not very good with money. They make bad decisions, and then often even worse decisions. They blow all their income, max out credit cards, drink or do drugs, show up late for work and get fired, live off the system, make miserable health choices, etc. What about *those* people who are just trying to get a free ride?

Fair enough. But if we only intercede for those who deserve it, we will never intercede at all. Waiting to help the so-called "deserving poor" is just one more excuse keeping us from doing what we should be doing simply as people of conscience. For the Jesus-followers, there's another layer: if God only interceded with those who deserve it, God would not intercede for any of us. From God's point of view, we're all equally deserving, or undeserving.[9]

The Soloist

ARIC

Steve Lopez was just looking for a story for his column in the L.A. Times when he first took interest in Nathaniel Ayers, the homeless musician who would change his life. He was intrigued to learn how a Julliard-trained cellist from Cleveland ended up sleeping on the streets of Los Angeles. In the interest of gaining Ayers' trust so he could learn the whole story, he found himself drawn into a

---

9. Romans 3:21–24.

relationship that would eventually become the subject of a book and a film featuring Robert Downey Jr. and Jamie Foxx.

The film received mixed reviews. As of this writing it sits at 56 percent (rotten) on rottentomatoes.com. Surprisingly, it got these mixed reviews despite widespread acclaim for the performances of the lead actors, who were both at the top of their popularity. There was buzzing. The word "Oscar" was dropped. Ultimately, what audiences and critics didn't like about the film was the open-ended plot. The movie centered on a relationship, not an event, and at the end of the film you aren't sure anything has been resolved.

In the film, Lopez tries to help Ayers get off the street and seek treatment for his schizophrenia. It doesn't go smoothly. Audiences would have loved a feel-good movie that ended with Lopez "saving" Ayers from his demons, and though Ayers is living in an apartment at the end, you aren't confident that it will last. Audiences would have even enjoyed the standard reversal of the savior plot, as in the movie Rain Man—*if Ayers had ended up "saving" Lopez—but Lopez is just as much of a flawed human being at the end as he was at the beginning. The only thing that has definitely changed for both men is that they have become friends.*

As Lopez says of his real-life relationship with Ayers, it has "always been a two-way street; it's not just me doing for him." Reflecting on what it means for me to intercede in the life of another person, it has to look like a two-way street, or else I am guilty of either codependence or paternalism. Instead of rushing in like a[10] superhero and rushing out just as quickly, I ask myself if I am willing to enter a relationship that may be complicated.

Intercession as a mutual relationship is not just the purview of the strong, or the highly skilled, or even those who think of themselves as courageous. It does require courage, but many who think of themselves as cowards are in fact brave. It doesn't require that you go out and start power-lifting and training to be a superhero. There are no superheroes, but there are opportunities for anyone to intercede.

Those Gritty Hebrew Women

There's more than one story in the Bible about interceding from weakness, but we're big fans of Shiphrah and Puah. Shiphrah and

---

10. Steve Lopez, *The Soloist: A Lost Dream, and Unlikely Friendship, and the Redemptive Power of Music* (New York: G.P. Putnam's Sons, 2008).

Puah are two midwives mentioned in Exodus; Hebrews working in Egypt under the rule of Pharaoh. Pharaoh sees that the Hebrews are becoming more and more numerous, even though they are being crushed down with hard labor, building storage cities to hold grain and other goods. Pharaoh, in the story, sees that he needs to make sure that the numerous Hebrews aren't able to get together enough men of fighting age to give him any trouble, so he commands that all male children are to be murdered at or shortly after birth.

Shiphrah and Puah, being midwives, are present for a lot of births. They are the ancient world's OBGYNs. As time passes, and Pharaoh isn't hearing of nearly enough infant deaths, he calls these two midwives before him. Imagine these women—members of an enslaved people, entirely at Pharaoh's mercy, tremblingly dragged into his vast throne room by armed guards.

He demands answers. What do they do? They intervene. They do not rise up and kill Pharaoh. They do not lead an armed rebellion the way they would if this was Hollywood. Rather, they come up with a clever lie. The Hebrew women are just tough, they say. They give birth too quickly, before the midwives are called, and they take their male children and hide them.[11]

We in the West are told similar stories even now—about how women in some developing nation don't feel pain in childbirth like American women do, and so they just give birth to their children and blithely continue working in the fields for the rest of the day. Shiphrah and Puah give the same story to Pharaoh. These are not like delicate Egyptian women, accustomed to luxury. These ladies are hardened slaves, and you just can't keep track of them.

It is a lie that Pharaoh is ready to believe—these are slaves, not the same kind of people as Egyptians. It's plausible that they would give birth more like animals, without as much pain, and then flee before their male children could be found and killed. In order to intervene, Shiphrah and Puah tell a plausible lie; they play on Pharaoh's prejudices. The two midwives also save their own lives, enabling them to do what they were doing in the first place—quietly helping Hebrew women, who are just like Egyptian women, enduring the painful and dangerous experience of childbirth, and keeping their male children alive.

---

11. Exodus 1:6–22.

The midwives took a huge risk. You go to jail for lying in a U.S. courtroom—one can only imagine the punishment in ancient Egypt for lying to Pharaoh. What they did was courageous, all the more so because it came from a place of weakness and not strength. Intercession does not require power. It simply requires a refusal to turn your back on need. Two women intervened on behalf of thousands of mothers and thousands of children. They bamboozled Pharaoh, and saved their own lives in the process. They didn't do this because they were powerful. They did it because the time came to act, and they did what they could, when they could.

Intervention isn't any more complicated than this—when the time comes to act, act in whatever way you can. Don't overestimate what you can accomplish, but don't hide behind underestimating either.[12]

Reaching into the Fire

NICK

They were on their way to school in Uttar Pradesh, India, riding in a Maruti van when a short circuit in the gas kit set the vehicle ablaze. The adult driver fled, abandoning the children to the fire. Eleven-year-old Om Prakash Yadav was able to get free from his seat in the front, but eight other children were still trapped. Despite the flames spreading to his arms and face, he went back into the van to help the other kids escape. He saved eight lives at the cost of severe burns causing him to miss a year of school, but if you ask Om Prakash if he would put his life in danger again if caught in a similar situation, he replies, "Every time."

There are many times in life when action just means more, when selfless acts of heroism don't come from those who don capes, making quick changes in phone booths, or from those who can leap buildings in a single bound. Instead, heroes are born in the blink of an eye, when, given a choice to turn and run or to step back into the flames, they choose the flames. Om Prakash said afterward, "I could feel fire burn my body, but

---

12. Another excellent story of interceding from weakness is the story of Esther, who risks death to draw the attention of the King of Persia to the plight of her people. When her uncle Mordecai is persuading her to act he memorably warns her, "Do not think that because you are in the King's house you alone of all the Jews will escape. For if you remain silent at this time, relief and deliverance for the Jews will arise from another place, but you and your father's family will perish. And who knows but that you have come to your royal position for such a time as this?" (Esther 4:12–14 [NIV]). These are good words for those of us who live comfortable lives. The cost we pay for failing to intercede is steep.

then I could hear the cries of my friends who were still caught inside the van. I threw my bag and entered to pull them out."[13]

Too often we feel like intercession is only for the powerful; it's only for someone more able-bodied, braver, or kinder than ourselves; but, in fact, chances for intercession are all around us. In this case the scars on his face will always be an account of the cost of his choice, but they do not diminish his spirit in the least. Young Om Prakash received the Sanjay Chopra award for his bravery, not because he is a person of extraordinary strength, but because he didn't allow his ordinary vulnerability to stop him from doing what was right.

And he is not alone. India's first prime minister, Jawaharlal Nehru, introduced the Sanjay Chopra awards in 1957 after he was taken by surprise by the brave act of a fourteen-year-old scout, Harish Chandra. The boy had saved hundreds by ripping a burning tent off of them after an electrical short ignited it. Since then, the heroic acts of the young ones in India have continued to be recognized. To date, 848 children have received the honor—600 boys and 248 girls.

No Hands but Yours

In the twenty-fifth chapter of the Gospel according to Matthew,[14] Jesus tells a story about intercession. He depicts himself as a shepherd separating out the sheep from the goats. The sheep he sends to the right and says they will be rewarded because they fed him when he was hungry, gave him water when he was thirsty, clothed him when he was naked, cared for him when he was sick, and visited him when he was imprisoned. The goats he sends to the left and says they will be punished because they didn't do these things.

This gets right to the beating heart of why we wrote this book. Your intercession is too urgently required for you to waste time on your knees, whispering words to a deity you imagine to be distant. God is right beside you, right now. Not in some mystical otherworldly sense, but in the hungry person you have a chance to feed; the thirsty person you could give a cup of water to; the naked person you could clothe; the sick person you could care for; the prisoner you could be visiting.

---

13. For more stories of the heroism of Indian children, read about other winners of the Sanjay Chopra award (http://en.wikipedia.org/wiki/National_Bravery_Award).

14. Matthew 25:31–46.

What is ultimately terrifying about the story in Matthew 25 is not that the goats get punished for their callous indifference, but that, because they didn't intercede, someone starved, someone got dysentery from unsafe water, someone shivered at night under a bridge, someone wept alone in a hospital bed, someone despaired for their life in a prison cell.

For the sake of the everyday hero that lives inside you, it is best if you assume that God will not intercede without you. There is no one about to come down out of the sky, cape fluttering, and relieve you of your responsibility to do what must be done.

***

Felicia hung up the phone. The local shelter and motels were all full. She'd spent more than half-an-hour trying to find a place for the family of six to spend the night other than their Ford Aerostar without success. She could hear her mother's disapproving voice in her head warning her not to do what she was contemplating. A million good excuses sprang to mind for why she should just send them on their way with apologies and maybe a bag of groceries. Instead she stood up and invited them back to her apartment. It would be crowded and inconvenient, but she couldn't let them stay on the street when she had an unused sofa-bed in her living room.

Experiments in Intervention

■ Commit to help the next person who asks you for help, whoever he or she happens to be. You don't have to save her life, or give him everything in your bank account, but you absolutely must do something concrete for this person. Afterward, congratulate yourself. You intervened when the majority of people wouldn't.

■ Choose a cause, something that really makes you sad or angry. Research concrete things you can do for that cause—more than just donating money; get your hands dirty. Commit to doing one concrete thing for your cause each month.

■ Make time to talk to, or at least e-mail or PM, each of your close friends and immediate family. Make sure that they know that you are willing to help them if they ever need it, understanding that there's a good chance that at least one of them needs help. When they ask, help.

Beg!

Emily sways during the hymns, lifting her hands to sing about God's power and God's control, God's might and God's glory. She basks in God's radiance, and it is almost enough to quiet the voice of shame inside her. While others make their requests aloud, she silently pleads for God's help. Her house is in foreclosure and she has no place to go. She's failing her children—failing to earn enough, failing to make the right choices. Each Sunday, and each night when she kneels by her bedside, she begs God for help. If her friends and neighbors learn she might lose her house, she'll die of shame. She begs the God of power and control to bless her the way God has blessed others.

The Myth of the Bootstrap

Autonomy is one of the highest values of American culture. We celebrate financial success and career advancement. We cheer mavericks and innovators who "break the mold" and "march to the beat of a different drum," and we all want to go out with Frank Sinatra's "My Way" being played at our funerals. The ideal of independence is exemplified in the way we build our cities with sprawling suburbs: 3,000 square feet of air-conditioned timber-frame construction per family, and a car for every driver in the household. It is why we worship athletes and movie stars whose individual achievements we honor with gaudy trophies and enormous salaries.

Meanwhile, we look down on those who are dependent on others to meet their needs. College students and young adults living with their parents "failed to launch." Those who utilize public services such as worker's compensation, welfare, or disability assistance are caricatured as lazy or dishonest. We have internalized this ideal of autonomy so thoroughly that the complaint frequently expressed by the elderly living in assisted-care facilities is that they are of "no use" to anyone. Being able to supposedly take care of yourself is such a defining value of our culture that when this ability is lost people see no more purpose in living at all.

There is a proverb that expresses this cultural myth: "Pull yourself up by your bootstraps." The delicious irony of this piece of popular wisdom is that it is impossible. Think about it. Bend over, take hold of the straps on your boots, and now lift yourself up off the ground. It can't be done. Yet we have made this ridiculous aphorism the cornerstone of our social values, and the result is pretty much what we would expect from a society trying to lift itself by its bootstraps—increasing effort and no progress.

In this climate of rugged individualism, begging is about the most humiliating kind of public failure we can imagine. Many of us choose to plunge deep into credit card debt before asking our own parents or friends for financial assistance. How much further would we be willing to privately self-destruct before admitting our desperation repeatedly to total strangers? The very word *beggar* is an antiquated-sounding slur, something that belongs in a Charles Dickens novel and not the twenty-first century, in which people carry mobile phones that are portable computers more powerful than the system that put humans on the moon.

Or maybe "beggar" fits perfectly, since we have exponentially increased the power of our microprocessors, but the way we respond to people in need is pretty much unchanged from Dickensian times. Check out the line on the first of the month for people receiving public assistance of some kind—or try applying for it yourself. The experience is replete with various kinds of humiliation and misery, and that's not even discussing the fact that on the news every night you are castigated as a lazy social parasite.

Begging in America is misery. In the most powerful and affluent society in human history, we only grudgingly treat people in need like human beings, and then only minimally so. Even brushes with the begging life are painful in our dysfunctional society.

A Box from Friends

DOUG

I've never outright been on the sidewalk shaking my coffee cup so the change rattles, but I've had multiple times in my life when I've had to depend on friends and family for basic needs. Every time, it's been painful, because I just don't have a way to ask for help that doesn't make me feel like a lazy freeloading loser-at-life. Even working six jobs at one point, having to ask for help tore me up inside.

The first time was when my wife and I were living in our first apartment. We had run out of money, and still had a month before we were scheduled to move to California. My wife had just had surgery, and we both had been laid off from our minimum-wage jobs. I vented on Livejournal (back when Livejournal was a thing) about the situation we were in, not really knowing what to do. We had already asked our parents for help with things like the deposit on the apartment and a computer—we felt like they were tapped out, or, at the very least, tired of bailing us out.

A few days later, a box arrived, addressed from a friend of mine. Inside was a note from a number of our friends and a ton of nonperishable food and gift cards to places like Subway. We stood in our living room looking at this box and cried. The pain of being in need and the joy and relief of having that need met by people who cared for us collided, and the impact was tangible.

When conversations about things such as begging break out, I am sometimes reminded that, as a white middle-class male, I am swimming in privilege. True enough. I've also had to beg, in my own way, for thousands of dollars of help over the years. The real privilege is that I have the resources, spread amongst my family and friends, that I can draw upon. Almost everyone I know who is around my age (early 30s) is in a similar situation. I know for a fact that without that privilege, I may very well be homeless, not because I didn't work hard or because I made bad choices, but just because when bad luck strikes all at once, and you have nowhere to turn, that's it. Now you're a beggar, and America looks down on you.

The Last Become First, and the First Become Last

There was once a rich man—he lived in a big mansion and had plenty of servants and a car for every day of the week. He had servants to clean his house and raise his kids and even do his taxes for him.

Outside his gated community was a poor man named Lazarus. He had a skin disease that made him ugly to look at, and you wouldn't want to touch him. Only the occasional stray dog would come to lick his wounds. Every day he would beg, and, every day, the rich man with all the servants would ignore him. He'd hide his face behind his morning copy of *The Wall Street Journal* while his driver drove him to work, or he'd sneer and think, "My taxes are paying for this guy to lay around? A travesty. Surely he's reducing our property values—maybe I can get the police to clear him away." But the poor man always came back, thinking maybe one of these "job-creators" might toss him some spare change.

One day, the rich man died. None of us are too big to fail in the end. His funeral was attended by CEOs, county commissioners, city council members, and party officials. There was weeping. There were speeches. When he died, though, he didn't like how he ended up. No streets of gold, no one in white robes handing him a harp and a halo. Just heat and darkness, thirst and loneliness.

Lazarus died as well, finally succumbing to his wasting disease and to privation and exposure. At the hospital where he was declared dead, no one came to claim his body, so it was claimed by the city after a few months and incinerated. Lazarus, though, when he died, was welcomed into a place of love and acceptance and life ever-after. He experienced the joy and care and dignity that was denied him in life.

The rich man felt too much like a servant, uncomfortable and kept in the dark and ignored, and he didn't like it one bit. He cried out, demanding, "Send that guy who used to beg outside my neighborhood with some water, and some food. Surely he can work now, since he never worked when he was alive." The answer was silence. The rich man had no servants here. He became afraid—he thought of all the well-to-do men and women he used to golf with and share cigars with and laugh about how great life was with servants and comfort and power. He cried out again, "Please! At least send that beggar to my friends, let them have a dream or something, to let them know that this is how it is! There must be a way out—I'll pay anything! Please just warn my family and friends!"

But there was just more silence, and loneliness, and heat, and darkness.

The rich man in that story is a true believer in the Myth of the Bootstrap. He's convinced himself that he is powerful, and others are weak, because he is smart and works hard and deserves what he has.

Hopefully Lazarus doesn't buy into the same myth, but more than likely, he does. He probably wakes up every morning hating himself, thinking, "What is wrong with me?" when he sees rich people drive past, ignoring him, stepping over him like a large but harmless insect. The Myth of the Bootstrap validates the false dignity of wealth, and it strips dignity away from the poor.

Begging in the face of the Myth of the Bootstrap is not just an act that brings humiliation—it is also an act of courage. Many people who have deep and abiding needs do not have the courage to make those needs known. They grit their teeth, play the rich man's game, and just accept the fact that they don't deserve to win. Their fear of being seen as losers and failures overwhelms their ability to tell the truth about what it is they need.

This story demands a different perspective. Lazarus is not a loser or a failure. Lazarus is the protagonist. Lazarus is the righteous one. Lazarus is the one Jesus invites us to identify with.

The beggar is the hero.[1]

The Privilege of Poverty

The heroism of begging is not our insight, of course. The tradition of voluntary poverty is a thread running right through Christian tradition back to the earliest days of the Church. Many of the most famous and lauded exemplars of the faith lived lives of austerity and simplicity. In some cases they gave up fortunes to become mendicants—beggars, living off of the generosity of others and the provision of God who tends to the lilies of the field.

One of these was a young girl named Clare. She was a runaway. Like a heroine from a Shakespeare play or a romance novel, she snuck out a window on a moonless night to escape an arranged marriage and the wrath of her very wealthy family. She met a humble friar[2] at a prearranged place. He cut her hair, exchanged her silk gowns for a coarse robe, and absconded with her to a convent. The friar helped her because she had begged him to teach her to live "in the manner of the gospel."

---

1. Luke 16:19–31.
2. This humble friar was Giovanni Francesco di Bernardone, better known as Francis of Assisi.

It was a passion she never lost her entire life, but in that moment it was particularly urgent because she knew that the kind of life she was called to live was radically different than the life of a Countess, even though she didn't yet have a clear picture of what that life to which she was called was like. The friar gave her an instruction: "Live according to the second evangelical counsel": poverty. Clare knew that she would forever renounce possessions. A holy path was laid out before her.

Clare had a fierce will. She fought off the angry attempts of her family to drag her from the religious life and she insisted on being moved from the Benedictine convent, where she was originally hid, to a place where she could follow a stricter rule of life. At San Damiano she was made abbess, over her objections, and she led the community there in committing to communal poverty. They would own nothing, either as individuals or as a collective. They would fast, eating no meat, every day of the year except the feast of the Nativity. Their clothes would consist of a simple robe, a linen cord with four knots, and cloth sandals. As women they were not able to be itinerant, so they would depend on what the friars could beg on their behalf. They would live off the charity of beggars.

In 1228 the Pope Gregory IX visited San Damiano and pressed the sisters there to accept some goods for storage to protect against unforeseen hardships, but Clare resisted. Gregory, thinking that Clare was afraid to violate her vow of poverty, offered to absolve her of the vow, to which she replied, "Holy Father, I crave for absolution from my sins, but I desire not to be absolved from the obligation of following Jesus Christ."

Nothing Glamorous

As inspiring as Clare's story may be, we will miss the point if we canonize her and set her aside as holy. If society has tended to marginalize and oppress the poor, the church has often accomplished the same result by romanticizing and idolizing poverty. If Clare becomes a mere saint in our eyes, we will miss her brokenness, her essential humanity, which is what makes her a truly compelling example. Her conviction was lived out in a self-destructive way that is not something to hold up as holy.

Almost all her life Clare suffered various infirmities associated with malnutrition—including, most famously, her bad eyes. Late in her life she could hardly leave her cell she was so often weak, and her vision so poor. Lying in her bed she hallucinated visions on the walls of her cell. She saw the mass and participated in the Eucharist in that way, from isolation. All of this most likely stemmed from her increasingly zealous fasting. They didn't diagnose it as such in her day, but she shows all the signs of someone suffering the eating disorder *Anorexia Nervosa*.[3]

Then, as now, the key words of the anorexic are "control" and "willpower." No one had an inner strength of will to compare with Clare of Assisi, but there is nothing glamorous about this kind of strength. It is a strength that inflicts a terrible kind of helplessness on friends and family members, who can only watch as their loved one starves. They watch as their protests go unheeded, as muscles wither and organs falter and eventually fail altogether. This is a strength that betrays a deeper weakness. Clare, far from being an example of perfection, was a very sick woman, and this is what makes her an acceptable icon of Christ. It is her need, not her fortitude or independence, which makes her Christlike.

It is important that we do not romanticize the very real and devastating effects of poverty. There is nothing noble about starvation or disease, or the misery these things bring to human lives. If we seek for ourselves the pious appearance of poverty, then we have turned it into just another luxury or status symbol, and we condemn ourselves as hypocrites. The point isn't to make a show of your fasting by disfiguring your face in public,[4] making a pretense of vulnerability. The point is to be vulnerable.

Jesus tells a story about a desperate woman. She is being persecuted and, since she is a widow, she has no one to protect her. She goes to a judge who is indifferent to her plight and she begs him for justice. He ignores her. He doesn't care. She keeps knocking on his door all day and all night, begging him for relief. Her need is overwhelming. Eventually the cruel judge gives in under the constant pressure and grants her justice. Jesus says that if even a corrupt judge eventually caves to genuine need, won't God rush to meet the needs of God's children?

---

3. The possibility that Clare of Assisi suffered with the eating disorder Anorexia Nervosa was the subject of an opera "Anorexia Sacra" by Line Tjørnhøj, blending extracts from Clare's writings as well as modern lyrics.

4. Matthew 6:16–18.

Once again the beggar is the hero of the story. Jesus commends those who bravely expose their need to the world.[5]

The Ambivalence of (Others') Need

NICK

I remember when I worked in San Francisco near Golden Gate Park. When I was on-call, we were given a small stipend to go buy dinner from a restaurant in the neighborhood because the cafeteria was closed. I used to walk down to the McDonald's, and every time I would go in to order something I would pass one of a few different homeless men who lived in the park. They would always ask me for spare change, or if I had anything I could give them—I in my dress pants, shirt, and tie; they in their hand-me-down pairs of jeans that were too big and needed a couple of washings to smell like pants again.

Why is it that I feel a lot more comfortable texting ten dollars to the Red Cross to support the earthquake and tsunami recovery efforts in Japan, or tornado recovery efforts in the Midwest, than giving that guy my ten dollars? I seem to relate only tangentially with people in need who are right in front of me, but I respond with great fanfare, riding to the rescue for victims of the latest natural disaster. I heap the blame for being homeless on top of an already distraught person, while all the time seeing "need" as something that only millions of dollars and massive fund-raisers can solve.

Each time I would round that corner toward McDonald's, I always knew I had a choice to make. Sometimes I got out my wallet and handed them something, sometimes I bought an extra cheeseburger that I would hand them on the way out. But mostly I avoided the need. I walked to that corner for more than a year, and I never once learned their names or their stories. What would have happened if I had enacted Jesus' commandment to give to anyone who asks of you?

Crumbs for the Dogs

Followers of the Way of Christ need to set aside the Myth of the Bootstrap. Jesus is not leading you to a place of self-sufficiency and strength. Jesus is walking a path of self-emptying and humiliation. Jesus is lowering himself and summoning you to be emptied of ego, to silence the voice that tells you that your worth is proportional to your productivity, and hear instead his pronouncement that vulnerability

---

5. Luke 18:1–8.

is honorable. Need is holy. Begging is an act of courage and sacred dignity.

This is a message that Christians who have spent abundant time training themselves to be "Good Samaritans" need to hear. We are well prepared to see the honor in being generous, in being heroic, and being the savior. We are less prepared to see the beauty of accepting help, admitting our weakness, and receiving grace. Everyone celebrates a knight in shining armor, but few admire a damsel in distress.

But it was a damsel in distress who taught Jesus the dignity of begging. He was staying in a home at the very edge of Israel near the city of Tyre, a Gentile port, when a Greek woman found him and literally threw herself at his feet. Weeping, she told Jesus that her daughter had gone mad, possessed by a demon. She begged him to heal her daughter. Jesus, in one of the strangest and cruelest moments in the gospels, doesn't grant her request. On the contrary. he insults her. He says, "First let the children eat all they want, for it is not right to take the children's bread and toss it to the dogs"

The children Jesus is referring to are the people of Israel. Jesus is saying that his gifts of healing and exorcism are intended for Israel and not for people like this Greek woman, whom he calls a dog—a *bitch*. This story gives preachers fits trying to explain why Jesus would behave so callously to a person obviously in desperate need, and rightly so.

Consider this scenario: a local congregation decides to start a food pantry. Before they open there is some discussion among the members about what the rules of the pantry will be. Can anyone get food? Do they have to provide identification? Is there a limit to how often they can come to the pantry? And so on. Being gentle-hearted people they decide to welcome anyone without identification on a first-come, first-served basis.

Very shortly after they open the pantry, some of the volunteers notice some customers coming again and again. Some customers refuse healthy foods, which they don't like, but are eager for the day-old donuts the supermarket donates. Volunteers learn that one of these customers who seem picky about their food is employed, and they've seen this customer talking on a cell phone. The volunteers begin to whisper that if people can afford cell phones, they should be able to afford to feed their families. The church begins to feel that its benevolence is being taken for granted and previously enthusiastic volunteers start to sour on the project.

Eventually, someone says that they need to revisit the guidelines for the pantry. A tense meeting is held in which some leaders argue for keeping the pantry as it is, while others demand more rules to ensure that the food is going to the right people. It is decided that every customer will now have to fill out a form with his or her personal information, and visits will be restricted to a monthly basis. They hope this will take care of the scammers.

It is a vain hope, unfortunately. No matter how many regulations are put in place, some of these volunteers will always feel that their generosity is being abused. The source of this feeling is not in the behavior of the customers in the pantry, but in the unacknowledged belief of the church members in their own superiority. They understand themselves as benefactors conferring their gifts on the less fortunate, a self-image that requires that they carefully discern the worthy recipients from the unworthy. It wouldn't be right to toss the children's food to the dogs.

If Jesus' insult phased the Greek woman, she didn't let it show. "Lord," she replied, "even the dogs under the table eat the children's crumbs"

To say the air must have been charged after this retort is an understatement. Jesus engaged in countless public disputes with lawyers and scribes, educated men accustomed to winning their debates. They threw everything they had at him in an attempt to embarrass and discredit him: highly technical interpretations of Torah,[6] legal and political conundrums to which a wrong answer could mean trouble with Rome,[7] and even baiting polemical traps with real human lives in the balance.[8] Jesus passed every test. He beat every argument. He won every debate. Until this woman showed up.

"For such a reply," he answered her, "you may go; the demon has left your daughter" Jesus concedes. He gives her what she asked for. He accepts public humiliation while she is vindicated. She goes home

---

6. Jesus disputes publicly with the Pharisees about Torah interpretation on several occasions. On one occasion he persuasively argues that correct observance of the Sabbath allows for the hungry to be fed and the sick to be healed (Matthew 12:1–14).

7. Mark 12:13–17.

8. John 8:1–11.

to find her daughter lying in bed. The demon is gone. Once again, the beggar is the hero of the story—even a story that includes Jesus.[9]

The solution to the above congregation's problem with the food pantry doesn't lie in any rule or system for discerning the worthy beggars from the unworthy ones. Budgets and logistical considerations are how we work out our morals, but the moral commitment comes first. If our commitment is to understand the beggar as holding the position of honor, then we will find solutions that reflect that belief. It is the one in need who has the truly precious gift to offer: the opportunity to serve.

Curry for the Sangha

ARIC

"They can't agree." This was the best our translator could do for us with the last attempt our Thai hostess had made to explain why we wouldn't be serving any meat to the saffron-robed monks of Wat Pra Singh. We had made a vegetable curry and rice and were prepared to schlep it in the back of several open-air bicycle taxis (called tuk-tuks) to downtown Chiang Mai, where the community of monks, the Sangha, would be making their daily plea for alms. A well-intentioned member of our group had purchased some chicken to put in the curry, but was told we couldn't use any meat.

Theravada Buddhists aren't strict vegetarians. Most understand the first precept, "Refrain from taking life," to prohibit killing animals for meat, and the monks would never cook meat for themselves, but one of their sacred texts, the Jivaka Sutta, explicitly instructs them to accept whatever is offered in the giving of alms without distinction. Our hostess was trying to explain to a group of English-speaking students that different monks work out the conflict between these two rules in their own way. Some monks happily eat the meat they receive in alms, which they wouldn't otherwise be allowed to eat. Some refrain only if they have reason to believe the animal was killed specifically to feed them. Still others politely refuse any meat offered to them.

"They can't agree."

So we would save them the need to wrestle with their consciences. We would provide them a delicious vegetarian meal.

As I spooned the yellow curry over another heap of rice in a simple wooden bowl, the monk before me wai-ed, and I returned the gesture,

---

9. Mark 7:25–30; Matthew 15:21–28.

making sure to keep my head lower than his. He was the one begging for his lunch. I was the one receiving the gift.

Beggar God

To paraphrase the former South African minister Andrew Murray,[10] we often try to forget our weakness: God wants us to remember it, to feel it deeply. We try to conquer our weakness and be freed from it, while God wants us to rest and even rejoice in it. It is our weakness, heartily accepted and continually realized, that gives us our claim and access to the strength of the one who said, "My strength is made perfect in weakness."[11]

God is our example of this sacred weakness. God took on flesh and blood in Jesus Christ, entering into the world through a scandalous situation in a little town in the middle of nowhere's-ville. When the time came, God set aside the divine nature, something of eternal and everlasting value, to become "nothing." God took the position of a servant, a beggar. In the ultimate act of humility, God came to dwell among us not in strength, but in weakness.[12]

The one revealed in Jesus of Nazareth is a Beggar God who straightforwardly proclaims "whatever you do to the least of these my brothers and sisters you do to me."[13] It has been the tragic conviction of countless missionaries and followers of the social gospel that when we proclaim the good news and help the needy it is we who are serving as icons of Christ, when instead we should approach our labor as supplicants seeking the face of God. Jesus calls us to the work of service because it is there that we meet him face to face. Jesus lives and walks the earth incognito in the skin of every child begging for food, every man begging for a drink, every stranger begging for a place to sleep, every family begging for clothes, every invalid begging for companionship, and every inmate begging for a visitor.

God is the beggar, which means that if we have in our lives a genuine need that compels us to reach out for help, then Jesus wears

---

10. Andrew Murray (1828–1917) was a minister of Scottish descent in the Dutch Reformed Tradition in South Africa who published over 240 books in his lifetime. This paraphrase is from *Andrew Murray, Abide in Christ* (Minneapolis: Bethany House Publishers, reprinted 2003).

11. Andrew Murray was paraphrasing 2 Corinthians 12:9.

12. Philippians 2:6–7.

13. Author paraphrase of Matthew 25:40.

our skin. The practice of begging is the discipline of dwelling in our need. It is the art of perfecting strength through weakness. We do it, not because it is comfortable or comes naturally to us, but because it is what God does.

Jesus is alive and in need. He is the amputee in line at the soup kitchen, the pregnant woman digging for food at the landfill, and the man sleeping off a hangover on the park bench. Jesus is enthroned at the right hand of the Father in glory—his throne is a cardboard box, and his glory is an old coffee mug that he holds out for your spare change.

***

Aiden was used to hearing the word "sorry." That's how everyone was telling him no: the banker who refused him a personal loan because of his student debt load; the stores, restaurants, and businesses who told him there were no jobs available; his landlord when asked if he could get one more week's extension on the rent. Now his few possessions were packed into his car and he pulled into the church parking lot. These people had been like his family while he was growing up. He hadn't visited in a while, but now he was coming to beg for their help. He prepared himself for another "sorry" from the pastor, mustering as much dignity as he could. If it came to it, he would sleep in his car in front of the church until they helped him.

Experiments in Begging

■ Commit to one day when you will not eat or drink anything that is not free or given to you freely. When you receive, do so graciously. When people respond to your asking with hostility or confusion, remember that they don't know you are trying to give them a gift.

■ The next time you see someone begging, go grab a couple of meals and come back and ask to eat with him or her. It'll be awkward, and they may very well say no, but, if possible, actually take time to listen. If he seems crazy, think of how hard it would be to get your life back together with a mental illness. If she seems drunk or high, remember how hard you find it to deal with your problems, and you have enough food and a place to sleep at night. If he smells bad, think how long you'd like to go without a shower. After the meal, thank the person, and don't ignore him or her the next time you walk by.

■ If you need help right now, go and ask for it. Stop putting it off; that's just your false pride. Put down the book and go ask. When you receive the help, just say, "Thank you." No excuses, no promises to pay them back someday. Reflect on the fact that you are very much like Christ in that moment.

Grieve!

Isaac comes in to work early, knowing he has a lot of making-up to do. As people come in, nursing coffee or pulling ear buds out of their ears, many of them come by his cubicle and offer their condolences. They know why he had to leave work early Thursday afternoon, and they were thinking of him over the weekend. How is he? How was the funeral? He smiles grimly and thanks them. His mind is on all the work he left undone, and he knows he only has today to catch up. His team is depending on him, and his boss is watching, and he doesn't really have time for all this.

A Question with No Answer

'If God is God He is not good,
If God is good He is not God;
   —Nickles, from the Prologue of *J.B.* by Archibald McLeish

In the above stanza, Archibald McLeish is making a point that is ancient and still unanswered, and which is likely unanswerable. It goes like this: if God is God—that is, if God is all-powerful, sovereign, and in control—then God is not good, because the world is full of needless suffering. Infants die of SIDS; tsunamis wipe whole cities off the map and sweep away thousands of lives; debilitating disease strikes good people and not-so-good people with impunity; nearly one billion human beings don't even have access to clean water.[1] If, however, God is good, then God is not God, not powerful, or not

---

1. For more information on the ongoing global water crisis: http://water.org/water-crisis/water-facts/water/.

able to intervene in the world, or not interested in doing so, which from our point of view is the same thing.

The idea, in essence, is that a good God who was powerful would not allow the world to be as it is. Even if we allow for the power of suffering to force needed change or to teach wisdom and virtue, or even just to punish sin, the amount of innocent, meaningless suffering in the world is inconceivable. It is hard to imagine what lesson a person learns dying from starvation, and 25,000 people die from starvation every day.[2] The same situation exists for crippling and deadly disease, warfare, and any number of calamities that simply cannot be justified as opportunities to learn or change. Some suffering can teach, but most suffering seems to be simply suffering—meaningless, tragic, entirely unjust. Who would allow that kind of suffering to go on, God or otherwise? If our hearts break when we look around ourselves at the world, how much more should God's heart break? And yet it continues.

Christians try to respond to this problem in various ways, none of them wholly satisfying. Calvinists, and most Traditionalists, essentially do away with God's perfect goodness. Focusing on God's power and control, they are forced to talk about God setting some people aside for suffering intentionally, while rewarding other people even though they cannot possibly deserve the reward. Underneath the theological language of double predestination, God is arbitrary. In a cosmic coin-toss unrelated to who you are as a person or what you will do in your life, God ordains that you will live in misery or bliss, on Earth as well as for eternity. The suffering we see, then, is not supposed to have meaning for a Calvinist. It is all God's plan, which we cannot understand. Calvinist theology essentially adopts this fundamental meaninglessness, and tries to account for it as part of the plan of a sovereign God.

On the other side, process theologians, Open Theists, and many other postmodern thinkers simply do away with God's absolute power. The answer for them is simple: God intervenes, but not in the ways we usually imagine—nothing dramatic or even direct. Rather, God intervenes to lure or draw people to the good, or to open possibilities that would not otherwise be open, or to respond in relationship but

---

2. Some names, faces, and numbers: http://www.poverty.com/.

with limited fore-knowledge and power. This is what McLeish means when he has the character Nickles say, "If God is good he is not God; Take the even, take the odd..." If God isn't able to intervene directly in a way that we can see, then what can we make of the stories in the Bible where God does just that? Even more, why does God matter? Who cares about a God who can't pull our irons out of the fire when the time comes? Is God simply a very helpful friend, well-meaning but as limited as any other friend?

There are other answers to this "problem of evil," the question of how the world can be as it is if God is both powerful and good.[3] The Calvinist and postmodern answers are simply the ones with which we, the authors, are most familiar. If there is a satisfactory answer to this question, though, we aren't aware of it. The issues of human suffering and the evil we experience from each other and from nature are so enormous that they defy comprehension, whether one believes in God or not, and Nickles makes a good point: it is easy to end there. Take it or leave it, and try to take some comfort in the moments of beauty we do find. Nickles' answer is no worse than that offered by many Christian theologies, and is much simpler. It accords with our experience of apparently meaningless suffering, in our lives and all around us.

In fact, this approach is quite similar to that of the biblical author of Ecclesiastes. The sage of that book begins by lamenting that everything is vanity—pointless, meaningless, empty. It is so because all of our lives are brief and full of suffering no matter what we do. He then describes how he sought happiness through all the paths available: he achieved wisdom, he accomplished great deeds, he accumulated property, he indulged all his senses with sex and wine and food. None of them resulted in lasting happiness. The sage ends up suggesting that when we accept the vanity of our various attempts to distract ourselves from suffering, we can be free to enjoy the time given to us, the company of friends, and the simple pleasures of life. In other words, accepting that there is no answer to our grief is actually the best answer.

---

3. The branch of theology that addresses the problem of evil is called "theodicy." In our opinion, the best work on this subject is Marilyn McCord Adams, Christ and Horrors: The Coherence of Christology, (Cambridge, U.K.: Cambridge University Press, 2006).

What comfort do we really expect from an answer, though? Would an answer change our basic human experiences of pain and loss? Would it hurt less to know that it was all part of God's plan, or that God is doing the very best God can, or that God doesn't matter and all we can do is hold onto the small comforts we can find? It isn't as if Calvinists, or postmodern theologians, or atheists cease to experience pain and loss. Loss comes to us all, whether we want it or not and whether we understand it or not—even the loss of God.

From the cross, Jesus cries, "My God, my God, why have you forsaken me?"[4] The absence of God is a basic Christian experience. This sense of abandonment is part and parcel to the Christian life. Rather than seek to escape it or explain it away, perhaps we are supposed to integrate it—to experience, without explanation, the pain of life and the fear of death.

Sitting in the Ruin

We don't choose whether to grieve. Grief comes, whether we want it or not, whether we are ready and willing or not. It is very common for people to grieve poorly, to feel that they "don't have time for this." At work you get an extra day or two for the funeral, and then it's expected that you come back at full productivity. Friends give you some time, but at a certain point they expect you to be "over it" and stop moping around. Family struggles don't wait for you to be done with grief, and they keep coming whether you are ready or not.

Grief is the emotional, spiritual, and physiological response to human loss. Grief takes on the form of sadness, anger, regret, guilt, depression, and preoccupation with thoughts of what, or who, you have lost. Many good books[5] have been written on grief alone, but in this case we are simply providing an introduction. Loss is inevitable, and with loss comes grief.

---

4. Jesus' cry of desolation on the cross (Matthew 27:46; Mark 15:34 [NIV]) is appropriately a reference to an earlier experience of extreme suffering. He is quoting the opening lines of Psalm 22. The absence of God isn't just a basic Christian experience. It is rooted in the universal human experience of isolation caused by suffering.

5. Nicholas Wolterstorff, *Lament for a Son* (Grand Rapids, Mich.: Eerdmans Publishing Company, 1987); C.S. Lewis, *A Grief Observed* (San Francisco: HarperSanFrancisco, 2001); David H. Kelsey, *Imagining Redemption* (Louisville, Ky.: Westminster John Knox Press, 2005); Shusaku Endo, *Silence* trans. William Johnston (New York: Taplinger Publishing Company, 1980).

This universal human experience requires a whole class of specialists in our society to help us deal with it—pastors and counselors and life-coaches and chaplains; psychologists and psychiatrists and nurses and doctors; psychics and mediums and everything in-between. Failing to enculturate ways to deal with grief, we instead fund a grief industry, and despite the time and money and various kinds of specialists, we do not grieve less.

In contrast to grief, there is mourning. In brief, mourning is the way that members of a culture consciously grieve. When we mourn, we engage with the grief, with the loss, mindfully and intentionally. In cultures with a strong tradition of mourning, significant time is given to a person undergoing this process. Weeping, wailing, and moaning may be expected—often there is special clothing, signaling that a person is in mourning.

In the United States, this period of outward mourning commonly lasts only a few hours—from an hour or two before the funeral to an hour or two after the burial. That is when we are allowed to wear black and weep. Then we go home, have some dinner, and get on with our lives. That's the plan, anyway. In reality, Americans are almost pathologically unable to mourn.

To mourn, to fully and consciously engage with the truth and pain of loss, is agonizing. It is something so difficult and frightening that incredibly successful people who are otherwise driven and aggressive risk-takers stereotypically shy away from grief. They end up in the telemetry ward of their local hospital with heart disease, or having escalating emotional outbursts interrupt their lives.

As a result of these various avoidance strategies, we tend to be dysfunctional in grief. It is ridiculous to expect a person to come out of an experience of grievous loss and simply return to work as if nothing happened. To imagine that we can suddenly adapt to a terrible experience, an absence in our lives, seems naive at best. Even giving slightly more time, "grief leave" for weeks or months, would be no guarantee. A society that is not able to deal with grief as an everyday experience is a dysfunctional society, as bad as a society that cannot deal with eating food or sleeping or working.[6] Grief cannot

---

6. Ironically, the United States is chronically obese, sleep-deprived, and overworked, as well as grief-averse.

be relegated to the fringes of our common life any more than it can be held at bay in our psyches.

A Lesson in Mourning

When I worked in an urban hospital in downtown San Francisco as a chaplain, part of our patient population was Cantonese-speaking Chinese immigrants. Whenever one of NICK *these patients died, usually in the ICU and sometimes in the ER, it was always a bigger event than other deaths. It was not unusual to have family members and Buddhist monks chanting sutras for 36 hours in the room with the deceased. Outside, the clinical director and nursing staff wrung their hands and worried about needing the currently occupied bed. In one memorable experience, a family was panicked because windows in American hospitals do not open, and yet in their tradition it is an imperative to open the window to allow the soul of the loved one to leave the room and return to their house. The wife shared with me about how for three years after the death of her spouse her loved one's soul would remain in their house. She told me that she would even continue to prepare meals and set a place at the table for him.*

These events always involved more noise than we are used to in the United States, as well as far more time. Caucasians like myself tended to be much more brief and orderly. About a half hour of tears and sharing memories, and then on with the transfer to the morgue and planning the funeral. The difference in effect, though, was dramatic. After 36 hours of chanting and weeping, a family knows for certain that they have paid their respect, and have done all they can for the departed to guide them into the afterlife and to demonstrate their love. While not at peace, their intentional mourning seemed to allow them to more healthily adapt to the loss, to absorb the pain mindfully.

Those more culturally similar to me, on the other hand, might continue to have mysterious effects for years. Having never spent time mourning, grief would sneak up on them and overtake them without their realizing it. Surprising emotions would burst out months and years later. They would "have issues," and would often need the help of professionals to work these issues out. Not to say that no Cantonese-speaking immigrants need similar help, but the difference was always striking to me, and I could see the profound value in noisy, active, public, and inconvenient mourning.

Dance in the Mourning

Even as disciples of an executed criminal who was a member of a subjugated culture, Christians are no less grief-averse than our neighbors. Compare the enthusiasm around Maundy Thursday or Good Friday to that surrounding Easter. *Fast forward past the cross to the Easter egg hunt, please.* Worship liturgies invite us to "weep with those who weep" and to "mourn with those who mourn," but we seem to imagine this involving a very limited investment of time—if we think about it at all. We only shed proverbial tears.

Perhaps engaging with grief directly was easier before Christianity was an imperial religion. The letters of Paul and the experiences of the early church were rife with persecution and suffering. Christian practice and living comfortably were mutually exclusive for Jesus' first followers. Historically as Christianity began to take on the shape of a formalized state religion, and shed its apocalyptic second temple Jewish roots, the level of suffering associated with belonging greatly diminished. With the conversion of Constantine and the establishment of bishops, elders, and deacons, the room for suffering and grief seems to have been systematically removed and replaced with a more triumphal religion.

Despite this dilution, it is noteworthy that mourning is built into the Christian liturgical year. Ash Wednesday, Maundy Thursday, Good Friday, and the less-commonly observed Holy Saturday are all liturgical moments of grief. Each encourages a different encounter with the grief at the heart of the gospel story—the whole of our complicity in evil that made the crucifixion an option in the first place. Not only the crucified God, but also the many others crucified by Rome, or executed by governments past and present, or killed in meaningless wars, or brought low by famine and thirst and disease.

What is God's answer to all of this suffering and evil? To *experience* it. God does not give a trite answer—God does not respond to Nickles' question in the way that Nickles demands, but does something far more profound. God's response to the suffering, sin, and evil in the world is to take it on, to have it break God's body and God's spirit, and to be crushed to death by its weight.

This is the heart of what it is to mourn—to walk into the open maw of grief, eyes open, and to stay there as long as we must to move through to the far side. In the Old Testament we are given the images of tearing one's hair, wearing sackcloth, and covering oneself with ashes—practices of public mourning. To mourn is to participate, naked and disheveled, in Christ's crucifixion, and to experience, perhaps, the hope of Christ's Resurrection, not through any kind of shortcut, but as a light we look to while we are in the midst of darkness.

Taking our cue from God, we are not merely to mourn our own losses, but to join others and mourn with them. In mourning, we enter into their suffering, into their pain, not with answers or any kind of fix, but with something far more costly and meaningful—our presence. It is one thing to say to someone, "This is what I think your pain means." Anyone who has heard those words when in pain can attest to how empty they can be. It is quite another thing to say to someone, "I will be with you as long as this pain lasts, and afterward as well, and I will help you however I can." Nobody gets an easy answer, but nobody has to be alone.

The Hilarity of Breast Cancer

Tragedy plus time equals comedy. That is the usual formula, but when comedian Tig Notaro stood up before the audience at Largo Nightclub in Los Angeles on August 3, 2012, there was no time to distance her from her recent cancer diagnosis.

ARIC

She was, as she said herself, still at "tragedy." That didn't keep her from delivering one of the most hilarious twenty minutes of standup that I've ever heard—not in spite of her tragic experiences, but because of them.

"Hi. I've got cancer. How are you?" She started her set nonchalantly and continued from there to delve fearlessly into the experience of being diagnosed with breast cancer, shortly after recovering from a debilitating bacterial infection, going through a rough break-up, and right before her mother died suddenly in a freak accident. The hospital sent her mom a customer-service questionnaire after she'd died, asking how her stay at the hospital had been. "Well," Tig deadpanned, "She died. So...not good," and you can't help laughing even if you also want to cry a little, and call that hospital to give them an earful for their insensitivity.

What Tig teaches us as she gets us to laugh about her flat chest, and the pain of a biopsy, and the awkward "funny cancer greeting cards" her friend shows her, is that there is humor even in the darkest and most tragic of situations. Humor isn't the opposite of grief; they are intimately connected. We laugh in the midst of our tears, and when we can't cry anymore, when our tears have finally dried, we've gained perspective. Laughter isn't just medicine, it is also protest, and acceptance, and solidarity, and wisdom. Sometimes grieving properly means recognizing how funny breast cancer can be.

The Lost Art of Lamentation

Lamentation is similar to mourning in that it is an intentional way to experience, express, and move through grief. Like mourning, there are a wide variety of cultural practices around lamentation, and, like mourning, lamentation is not a very common practice in industrialized societies. There is plenty of complaining, to be sure, but lamentation is more than that. Where mourning is engaging directly with grief, lamentation goes a step further to call out the injustice that is the cause of so much grief. It is the acknowledgment not only of the pain of loss but also of the unfairness of so much apparently meaningless suffering in our lives and around us.

Death is the enemy. Loss is painful. We can say to ourselves, "In Christ, loss is gain!"[7] all we want—the brutal facts remain unchanged. Even a "natural" death, an unavoidable loss, is a victory for entropy. There is nothing more valuable than a conscious being, and there is no way for any conscious being to end up as anything but fertilizer. On a long enough timeline, every mote of matter and every wave of energy will degrade into a cold emptiness. Energy is changed, and not lost, but it degrades steadily on a cosmic scale. Matter is not lost, but it is rapidly flying apart and disintegrating, or collapsing into black holes where even information is destroyed. This is our life, and this is our universe: it ends.

In saying this, we leave aside the incalculable destruction and loss that occurs as a result of evil. Natural evil arises in the form of natural disasters, diseases, and organisms that want to kill and eat us. Moral evil arises in the form of starvation, rape, betrayal, war, oppression, and lies. Heaped upon the baseline tragedy and suffering in the universe is the suffering and tragedy that we, conscious beings, contribute. To lament is to give voice to this core injustice—to tell it like it is, and not dress things up with flowery language or contorted justifications. It is to call to the carpet all that deserves our anger and our rage.

The story of Job is a story of lamentation. God allows Job to be stricken beyond all endurance, despite the fact that he is described

---

7. Author paraphrase of Philippians 3:7–9

as a righteous person, someone who deserves no such treatment. His wife and friends all endeavor to convince Job that, somehow, he deserves what happens to him, but he holds out, demanding that God answer for what has happened to him. He slaps aside their feeble and desperate attempts to moralize and theologize, to blame the victim and prop up the idea that people get what they deserve in the end— that God's justice looks like the balancing of the cosmic ledger.

God's reply is brutally honest: there is no answer, and no explanation. Out of the whirlwind God's message is very clear: the injustice is there, and there is no good explanation. The answer that Job so ardently sought is simply not there to be found.

Sometimes our job is to help those who are in the midst of grief find their voices for lamentation; to recognize and protest unjust suffering; to provide a place for the grieving to be heard and not judged; to offer an ear to listen in desperate times, without moralizing or theologizing, without falling back on platitudes in fruitless attempts to soothe their righteous indignation. We can even join them in "eating tears."[8] In Psalm 80, the people of Israel are suffering, and to convey the depth of the people's anguish, the psalmist uses the stark phrase *lechem dimah,* or "bread of tears." They are eating tears, and being served tears to drink. In the absence of any possible explanation, we can instead shake our fists at injustice, sit with each other in solidarity, and eat the bread of tears together.

Beauty in Grief

Poetry is one of the most powerful ways of expressing grief, and among the most evocative of poetic forms is the jisei, or Japanese death poem. I think it says something interesting about the culture of Japanese Buddhism that there is an entire genre of poetry written by those who are on the verge of death. The idea is that, when facing one's own death, it is possible to be more lucid and insightful, and the poem is a way to express this (hopeful) wisdom before it is too late. Examples will be better than my description, so here are two in translation from Yoel Hoffman's book Japanese Death Poems:[9]

---

8. Author paraphrase of Psalm 80:5.

9. Yoel Hoffmann, *Japanese Death Poems: Written by Zen Monks and Haiku Poets on the Verge of Death* (North Clarendon, Vermont: Tuttle Publishing, 1998)

Inhale, exhale
Forward, back
Living, dying:
Arrows, let flown each to
each
Meet midway and slice
The void in aimless flight
—

Thus I return to the
source.

     —Gesshu Soko, died January 10, 1696, at age 79

Spitting blood
clears up reality
and dream alike.

     —Senryu, died September 23, 1790, at age 73

DOUG

Maybe that gives you an idea. The oldest poems are more than a thousand years old, and the newest ones are being written right now by dying Zen Buddhists. It's worth noting, as an American, that in my country we shut dying people away in hospitals and nursing homes. When we talk about death, about the cost of healthcare, about anxiety, and about death-rate statistics. We don't talk about the insight available to us, much less the beauty.

What's the point of being afraid of death? What does the dread buy us? Jesus would say, "Nothing at all," and though I fear death, I'm inclined to agree.[10] In these death poems, I encounter beauty and insight and even a lot of wry humor. Mindfulness of death—my death, your death—can sharpen my experiences of beauty, and even increase my zest for life. The truth is that I will die whether I experience beauty and live zestfully or not—but thinking about my own death can bring things into sudden focus, even now as I am quite alive. As I someday face my own death, and before then face the deaths of many people I love, I hope that I can approach death and grief with the expectation that I will find wisdom, insight, and perhaps even joy—or, at least, wry humor.

---

10. Luke 12:25–31.

An Epilogue for Tears

Grief, mourning, and lamentation are temporary. This is one reason that we can bring ourselves to engage in these practices—they represent a reality of suffering and evil and injustice that is painful and destructive on a cosmic scale, but that is also not the last word. In response to the character Nickles, whom we quoted at the beginning of the chapter: God is God *and* God is good, and even so we have to "take the even and take the odd" in our brief lives. We do not only have the consolation of fleeting beauty—the leaves in the wood and the wind on the water—but the consolation of beauty that is the culmination of all things.

The writer of Revelation speaks of this beautiful culmination in which all evil is destroyed, all suffering ends, every tear is wiped away, and God's people live in the midst of a new paradise forever.[11] Grief, that temporary thing, is salved away. Mourning has no purpose, and there is nothing to lament.

For now, we must grieve because in grief we inhabit our own skin when loss strikes. To grieve is to be human; to grieve is to be vulnerable, to be helpless, to be caught in the midst of pain that is greater than the meaning we are able to grasp.

For now, we must mourn because in mourning we engage with the truth of our lives consciously. The pain of our wounding builds compassion and can even bring wisdom. To sit in the midst of ruin takes more courage than perhaps anything else in life; to mourn—to go intentionally into the ruin and to engage with it and understand it—even more so.

For now, we must lament because the world is not fair, and our hearts are supposed to be broken by the suffering and evil we experience. To lament, to feel undeserved pain and to give voice to both grief and anger, to raise a protest in the very moment when it seems no one could possibly be listening is nothing short of heroic.

For now, we do this because we are training our hearts to break when God's heart breaks. Why do our hearts break? Because we know that this is not how things are supposed to be. There is something better, something more, that is intended for us and for everyone

---

11. Revelation 21.

around us. We look forward to the time when we are made whole, when the world is made whole around us, and when tears will only be a memory.

Until then, we grieve.

***

The first people who come to the scene watch as first responders flood the building, leading terrified teachers and children out, putting up yellow tape, then collecting evidence as the sun goes down and the only lights are flashing red and white. They stay, share coats, bring food to distribute. Some come with candles, which they light, and place them in front of the main sign, beneath the mascot and the words, "Welcome back from winter break!" More join them with photographs and wreaths and pictures drawn by other children in town. Reporters come and go, but few can find any words to say into the cameras. They gather, amidst the candles and the memories, in the sun and in the rain, day and night. They gather together and hold onto each other as the nation argues about guns and violence and videogames and mental illness. They weep together and sit and stand, go home and return after work. They sing and are silent and talk to each other, while the nation forgets, moves on. The mayor comes, and pastors and rabbis and imams, and some Buddhists from another town. The set up a podium for their district representative, who gives a fine speech. She leaves, and they are still there. They weep together because they cannot forget, and they stand together in the sun and the rain so that no one else forgets the beautiful lives snuffed out, taken away, gone and never to return.

Experiments in Grieving

■ Write a letter to a dead loved one, listing all that you miss about this person. Say the things you wish you had said, and apologize for the things you wish you hadn't said. Leave it at the grave site, if possible.

■ We hope you don't, but if you suffer a loss, wear black for a full month afterward. Does this change your willingness to talk about the loss directly? What kinds of reactions do you get from others?

■ Set up an appointment with a funeral home, and meet with them and talk about plans for the end of your life. What kinds of things happen? What sorts of decisions do you need to make? What mistakes do people commonly make when facing the end of their lives?

■ When someone near you loses a loved one, ask if you can call them regularly. Call every day for six weeks. Ask how the person is, don't presume, and take the time to listen to the answers.

■ Fill out an Advanced Healthcare Directive. Think about what kinds of interventions you would want if something bad happened to you. Research what things such as CPR actually do to the body, and what it is like to be chemically paralyzed and on a breathing machine. Share this Advanced Directive with your immediate family—it'll probably lead to a pretty serious conversation you wouldn't normally have about death and loss.

Thank!

After she breaks the bread and pours the cup and says the words, the pastor lifts the chalice over her head. "The Lord invites all people to His table. We come from east and west, from north and south, to sit at Table with the Lord. This is the glorious feast of the Kingdom of God! All baptized believers are welcome here. Come, eat, and be filled." The members of Our Redeemer Church file out of their rows and make their way slowly to the front of the sanctuary as directed by the ushers in each aisle, just as they have done for a hundred years—all fifty of them, in a sanctuary that could seat two hundred easily. Caucasian, middle and upper-middle-class, with an average age of 67, they come; from east and from west, from north and from south, they come, take sips of grape juice from tiny plastic cups, nibble tiny stale bread cubes, and return to their seats in silence.

The Economy of God Is at Hand

If there is anything our lives teach us it is this: there are limits. There are limits to how fast you can run. There are limits to the amount of oil we can dig up from the Earth. There are limits even to enormous things, such as the number of helium atoms in our sun. Everything is limited. A word for this is *scarcity*.

Scarcity is a fact of life, whether individually or in life together. We must understand our limits, and use what we have as consciously and conscientiously as possible. As a society, scarcity comes to the forefront in our economic relationships. The idea that everything is limited becomes the idea that there is not enough to go around. The idea that I must get all I can, even at the expense of others, follows along inevitably. How can I ever be sure I will have enough? I must have more than enough, just in case.

The anxiety that scarcity creates means that we are all frantically scrambling for every scrap we can get our hands on, and the one with the most scraps at the end of the game is the winner. It is just like a game of Hungry Hungry Hippos,[1] only the losing hippos starve to death, or live their days in miserable poverty, and the winning hippo assumes he won because he deserved to win. The only certainty in a world of scarcity is that there will be very few winners and many losers, and no one likes to lose. The system uses this fear of losing to perpetuate itself. The idea is that the few winners will inspire the many losers to work harder, because we falsely suppose one is only poor through a failure of intellect or character.

In the United States, the story we tell ourselves is a story of growth. We imagine that the key to ending poverty, to ending hunger, to solving all societal ills, is continued growth. Growth is health—when the growth slows, we call that a recession, and we get very nervous. When that growth stops or corrects itself, we call that a depression, and we panic. We do all we can to promote growth, even when only a tiny minority of our citizens experience any benefit from that growth. We don't really care—growth is life, growth is health, and to see that growth slow or stop is to face the fear of death. As a result, we consume more, spend more, go deeper into debt, exploit more, and pollute more. We keep doing this until the system collapses, and then we turn a few knobs and get it up and running again.[2]

It is a deep irony that our concept of limitations leads us to seek a solution that is based on ignoring those limitations. The very scarcity that drives our economics exposes our growth-based economic system as not only ridiculous but utterly doomed. There is no chance whatsoever that economic growth will solve our problems in the long term. You cannot keep using more and more of limited resources and expect anything good to happen.

Deep down, many of us know this. We become desperate, fearful, and often violent. For some this means packing a bug-out-bag and

---

1. If you don't know what "Hungry Hungry Hippos" is, we mourn for your childhood.

2. This critique of modern capitalism is widespread, but one person who expresses it well is Naomi Klein, *The Shock Doctrine* (New York: Picador, 2007). There is also a documentary, released in 2009 with the same name, directed by Michael Winterbottom.

hoarding supplies in case of disaster. Others are driven to seek power through politics to protect their personal interests. The knowledge that fossil fuels must run out prompts us to fight wars and proxy wars wherever there is oil for the taking. Soon the limited supply of fresh water will cause similar wars all over the globe. Diminishing topsoil feeds famine and unrest; exploding populations press us closer together and shrink the space we can call our own.

The inevitable result of all of this is collapse. It is not a matter of whether collapse will come, it is a matter of when. No one who has ever looked at an exponential function can disagree—consumption is already beginning to outstrip the capacity of the Earth to safely support human life. We are fishing out the seas, draining nutrients from the soil, polluting the water, and raising the temperature every year. Over time, these things will get worse, and they will get worse at an increasing rate. The same technologies that will solve some of these looming problems will create new problems in turn, just as they have in the past.

This is our economy: an accelerating rush toward collapse, borne on the backs of the suffering poor, one generation stealing from the next, with the vulnerable always paying the greatest price. This is our economy, but it is not the only economy. God's economy is different in every way, and it is the only path to abundant life for all.

God's economy is a seed of revolution buried in the soil of the Church; if it takes root and blooms, it will tear our system apart and replace it with one that will not drain our lives away and doom our descendants. Unlike *our* economy, God's economy has a future, but the only way into that future is to preside over the death of our economy as it is now.

Rolling Jubilee

DOUG

It took Occupy Wall Street before anyone tried to live out God's Jubilee. In Leviticus 25, the Jubilee is described as a time every fifty years when all property will be returned to the original owners and all slaves will be set free. It is across-the-board debt cancellation—starting over from scratch with an economy that has no debt or debtors. I'm not aware of any clear evidence that this was actually practiced on a large scale in ancient Israel. If it had been, it would have had sweeping effects on every single person in that society—but they likely ignored it, just as we do.

Last year, something started as part of the Occupy movement, first in New York but inspired by movements all over the world. They call it the Rolling Jubilee.[3] The Rolling Jubilee is a nonprofit organization that receives donations and then uses those donations to purchase defaulted debts on the open market. They then cancel the debt they have purchased, and send the people a letter letting them know their debt has been cancelled.

That this act of charity can change a person's life for the better is obvious, but there has been a second effect, which is to reveal the ridiculous injustice of the debt system itself. The Rolling Jubilee regularly purchases debts at one-twentieth their actual cost, meaning someone's $10,000 debt can be purchased by a debt collector for $500. That's right, those people who hound you and call you at work and threaten to take you to court to make you pay your debt are looking at a 2000 percent profit margin. For Rolling Jubilee, what this unjust debt market has done is to make the donations they receive twenty times more powerful.

As of this writing, Rolling Jubilee has abolished 11.5 million dollars of debt. This is what it looks when our debt-driven economy is occupied by grace: people are set free and injustice is laid bare.

Communities of Enough

At the core of God's economy is not scarcity, but grace. In God, there is enough for everyone.[4] This message, perhaps more than any other, challenges us as modern and postmodern people in the developed world. Our whole lives we are fed the lie that continued growth is not only good, but it is what will save us. We are also told that there is not enough for everyone, and we are rewarded for ignoring the obvious contradiction in those two bedrock assumptions of our system. Let the next generations worry about the fallout—all's fair in market capitalism.

God's economy is different: it looks different, it feels different, and it calls us to different kinds of behavior. God's economy doesn't frighten with scarcity or promise unlimited growth; it rests on "enough."[5] Enough means that we have everything we need, and can make sure that everyone else has what they need, and the one who

---

3. www.rollingjubilee.org.
4. Micah 4:4; Isaiah 65:19–23.
5. Our concept of enough has been greatly influenced by Brené Brown, *Daring Greatly* (New York: Penguin, 2012).

gives the most away wins the greater share of joy and goodwill. In a context of enough, having more than enough becomes questionable rather than laudable.[6]

The core image of enough, for Christians, is in the Eucharist. In communion, we share in the opening salvo in the revolutionary overthrow of our economy. This idea was as frightening to the early church as it is to us now. In the Christian communities of Corinth, it was apparently all too tempting to simply replicate the world's economy in the Love Feast that Christians shared together. The wealthy and powerful would arrive early, eat all the best food, and then retire to their own part of the room, or their own rooms, to enjoy each other's company. It was like volunteers at a soup kitchen partitioning off part of the room and eating all the food before any of the poor arrive, treating it like the dinner parties they are accustomed to. This mirrored the situation at the time. Roman elites, like elites anywhere, loved to gather together to drink, eat, listen to good music, have sex, and lock their doors to the huddled masses of the poor. It seemed appropriate to simply perpetuate this system in the Love Feast, trading Christ's radical table-fellowship for the table-fellowship of the corrupt status quo.[7]

In the same way, it is tempting for churches and Christian communities now to lazily import their economies into their communal life. Churches have implicit, or explicit, dress codes, and people who attend in tattered or dirty clothing are looked down upon, or politely asked to leave.[8] Fundraisers to repair the pipe organ or recarpet the sanctuary are popular and successful, while fundraisers to support the local food bank or homeless shelters often fall flat, or raise pennies compared to every dollar spent on new carpeting. Racial divides are brought into church and, if anything, magnified— Sunday morning continues to be the most racially segregated time in American culture, because we simply apply to church the assumptions we apply to where we live: "That's a Black neighborhood, and over there is a White neighborhood, and that's where the Latinos live," and so on.

---

6. "Not to enable the poor to share in our goods is to steal from them and deprive them of life. The goods we possess are not ours, but theirs." —Saint John Chrysostom

7. 1 Corinthians 11:17–34.

8. James 2:1–7.

Communion is a chisel placed against the craggy face of our economic assumptions, and enough is the hammer blow that seeks to shatter them. In communion, there is always enough for everyone. That was what the churches of Corinth missed, and what got Jesus into so much trouble. Not only is there enough food, there is enough fellowship. There is enough grace. There is enough dignity. It may seem like an easy thing to plan to feed everyone who comes to the table, and a simple task for the more privileged in a community to wait to be served with the less privileged—but, to insist that the privileged forsake that privilege that they have in every other part of society, to invite the outsiders and the unclean and the sinners to break bread with them, to consciously overturn the racist assumptions of our larger society—those things go against everything our society teaches us. Those things are *communion*.

Consider this example:

One Sunday at the communion table, a pastor told her congregation that there was excess bread for the sacrament and encouraged everyone to take a generous helping. In truth, there was the same amount of bread as always, but she wanted to test a hypothesis. At the beginning everyone was taking large hunks of bread, but as the loaf was passed around the room people noticed that there was less and less of it. They began taking slightly smaller portions, and those who had earlier taken large portions held onto their portions and did not eat them. The last dozen or so people took very very small pieces of bread, but there was always more to pass down the line. No matter how small the loaf got, each person ensured there was enough to pass to the next person. When every person had been served, some of those with large hunks went and shared their bread with those who had received very small pieces. Everyone was fed.

The same thing would happen at most family dinner tables. As the food is passed and served, the diners look to their left and right to be sure that everyone is getting enough. Before someone scrapes out the last of the mashed potatoes, that person asks if everyone has had some. If a family like this were to have unexpected guests arrive, they would go to the kitchen and get out more food to be sure that they had enough. At that church described above, if they had completely run out of bread for communion, someone would have been running to the kitchen to get more, or even driving down the street to grab another loaf and bring it back to the church.

When communities embrace God's economy, the belief that there is enough for everyone moves from a conviction to a commitment. Everyone takes responsibility to ensure that it is indeed the case: that everyone's needs *are* met. When this is done, if the feeding of the 5,000 is to be believed, there is even food left over.[9]

"There is enough for everyone" is an assertion that has, in the past, earned those who said it exclusion, threats, torture, and even death. We who have power, and those few who have far more power, know on some level that our power derives from the idea that there is *not* enough for everyone. How else could we possibly justify allowing a single human being to go hungry, or to lack shelter or medical care, or the opportunity to learn and create art? The answer is that we could never justify those things, if not for scarcity. Even as the economy of God lavishes us with sustenance and dignity and grace, it also lays bare the injustices that make our lives possible, and demands that we care for those who lack what we have.

Food, not just Bread

NICK

One of the earliest conversations that eventually turned into the book that you hold in your hands comes from a favorite ministry of mine. The story is well documented in Sara Miles' book Take This Bread.[10] *It's one of the purest examples of gratitude that I have witnessed. Every Friday, right around their communion table, St. Gregory of Nyssa Episcopal Church in San Francisco lives out their theology of abundance by giving away free groceries to hundreds of hungry families. Fresh fruits and vegetables, rice, beans, pasta, cereal, and bread are peacefully and beautifully shared.*

While I lived in the Bay Area I had the pleasure of serving there on several Fridays, and I witnessed a food ministry that was, as Sara Miles puts it, "a vision of God's ridiculous, over-the-top abundance." It's a pantry run mostly by the very folks whom it served and continues to serve. Many originally came to get food, but then stayed to help out. It's food— fresh, wonderful food served directly off the communion table to feed all who come. The symbolism should not be glossed over: the Eucharist, Holy

---

9. The feeding of the 5,000 is the only miracle (apart from the Resurrection) that appears in all four gospel accounts (Matthew 14:13–21; Mark 6:31–44; Luke 9:10–17; and John 6:5–15).

10. Sara Miles, *Take This Bread: A Radical Conversion* (New York: Ballantine, 2008).

Communion, the Lord's Supper served each week from the same table as the food for the hungry.

Folks call St. Gregory's the dancing church because of the incredible mural that graces their worship space, in which the congregation dances its way around the altar to receive the body and blood of our Savior. I call it the dancing church because the most beautiful dance I've ever witnessed was how all were welcome to give and receive at this food pantry.

Table Manners

The anxiety created by scarcity makes us grasp and cling. Living into God's economy, the conviction that there is enough for everyone, means letting go. We have to begin to give freely. The practice of gratitude begins with generosity and grows increasingly reckless and joyful.

In one of Jesus' most famous speeches, he told his disciples to consider the flowers of the field.[11] They don't work or store up grain, but God makes sure they're cared for. Jesus told his disciples not to worry about food or clothing or material needs, that God would provide such things. He instructed them to set out on their mission with nothing but their coats and their staffs and to count on the hospitality of strangers for their daily bread.[12] It was an austere lifestyle, to be certain, but one that expressed profound confidence that there is enough for everyone. Jesus tried to turn his disciples away from anxiety and toward trust.

As a starting point, consider a commitment to some small form of random generosity. Buy the food or drink of the person behind you in line. Put money in other people's parking meters. Give to those who ask you for money. As you become accustomed to this commitment, increase it. It will be uncomfortable for a while. If the commitment is sufficiently serious, it will put you in the position of occasionally giving something away you would rather have used for yourself.

The randomness of the generosity is important. While there is definitely a place for calculated benevolence designed to do the most good for the largest number of people, we cannot teach ourselves gratitude by carefully measuring how and when to give and who is worthy of receiving. That type of strategic thinking reinforces our

---

11. Matthew 6:25–34.
12. Matthew 10:5–15.

perception of scarcity. It betrays our belief that even kindness has to be rationed.

When you are ready to get serious about living into God's economy, examine your possessions and lifestyle to see what else you may give away. Do you have more than enough clothing? Give it away. More than enough furniture? Give it away. More than one car? Give it away. Do you even need a car? Would a bicycle or public transit be enough? Do you have extra space in your home? Open it to someone in need of shelter. Invite friends and acquaintances to eat in your home often—even better, invite strangers to eat with you, for by doing so some have unknowingly entertained angels.[13]

What we are after is training ourselves to trust. Trust over time becomes joy as we discover we've stumbled onto the truth—that there really is enough for everyone—and this truth destroys our fear. Joy leads to greater generosity, which leads to deepening trust and more joy. This is the cycle of thanksgiving. The more we give, the more grateful we find ourselves for what we have been given, and the greatest thing we have been given is the opportunity to give.[14]

Suddenly, the psalmist's imagery of a cup overflowing makes sense.[15] Like excess liquid tumbling over the side of a goblet, the practice of gratitude becomes almost involuntary. It is a joyful reflex, not conditioned by what we have or what we lack, but by our trust in God's grace.

Tables of Bounty

ARIC

As a sixteen-year-old foreign exchange student in Rio De Janeiro, one afternoon I got lost wandering around the hills of that city. I didn't know it then, but I'd somehow turned down a long road that plunged through the heart of Rocinha, the largest favela (shantytown) in Brazil. When I was later safely returned to my host family, they gasped at my ignorance and good fortune to have avoided getting mugged.

Not only did I not suffer any misfortune, but a family of strangers spotted me, so obviously out of place, and took pity on me. They invited me into their home, which was a hodge-podge of brick and corrugated

---

13. Hebrews 13:2.
14. 2 Corinthians 9.
15. Psalm 23:5.

metal with a dirt floor. Their oldest son, Marcio, promised to give me a ride on his bicycle to the bus station and directions home, but first I had to stay for dinner. Their dinner was Feijoada, a kind of bean stew. It was not very good and it was not very much, but somehow it remains one of the most special meals I've ever had.

Years later, in Rome, I was invited to a Shabbat dinner at the home of some very well-to-do Italian Jews. They graciously shared their rituals with me, translating the Hebrew into English, and laughing good-naturedly at my poor Italian. Americans wish their Thanksgiving meals were this extravagant. Course after course of exquisite home-cooked Italian cuisine passed in front of me, along with limitless fresh-baked bread and bottomless wine. I stumbled into the streets of Rome that night so engorged I swear I didn't eat for days.

I would describe both of these tables, superficially very different from each other, as "bounteous." Both families went far beyond the duties of hospitality. They gave generously, without counting the cost, when there was no possibility of me returning the favor. There is simply nothing you can say to bounty like that except, "Thank you!"

God Is Thankful

The word we use to refer to gathering at Christ's table is *Eucharist*: literally, "thanks-giving" in Greek. Thankfulness is at the heart of the Eucharist, or communion, and we thankfully gather at Christ's table because it is, first and foremost, Christ who is thankful. It is tempting to think of God as always being the one who receives our thanks, but, in the upper room, when Jesus shared the meal that we took as our paradigm for communion, he began by giving thanks. That is to say, on that night *God* gave thanks.[16]

Thankfulness leads to the perception that "there is enough," and also to the generosity that flows from that perception. If I have enough, more than enough, then nothing whatsoever stops me from giving some of what I have away. We see this attitude in Jesus and in the spirit of self-sacrifice that animated many in the early church, and the connection between this self-giving love on the one hand and the hospitality of Christ's table on the other hand is not coincidental. Each fed into the other, and one guiding image was, and is, Jesus giving thanks as he broke bread on the night he would be betrayed.

---

16. Matthew 26:26; Luke 22:19.

In the same way that we project our economic assumptions on those with whom we share community, we project our ideas of power and authority on God. There is a common and deeply unfortunate view of God, wherein God is towering and distant, looming like a vast thundercloud, and seeking to inspire fearful and cringing obedience in humankind. In turn, we worship and give thanks to God, in the hope that we will appease God, or at least make God temporarily happy. We imagine God, arms crossed, glowering, saying something like, "Yes, worship me—it is the least that I deserve from you."

What about the image of a thankful God? Most Christians call God "Father," and if we knew of a father who was not thankful for his children, we would rightly look down on that person and wonder what was wrong with him. We would not expect that thankless person to be a very good father. How much more so can we expect God to be thankful for us?

God's thankfulness manifests in generosity. God is the gracious host. Jesus speaks of the host of a banquet for which the host has received many, many excuses about why invitees cannot attend. Everyone is too busy protecting what they have to attend. And yet the host keeps sending his servants back out onto the street to collect all who will come, searching high and low, because there is plenty of food and celebration to be shared.

Every advertisement, all of our media, almost everything in our culture strives to convince us we live in a world of scarcity and we have to fight for our share of prosperity, but God's economy is where grace and gratitude dance. We can choose to live into that reality, where everyone has enough—enough food, water, medicine, dignity, freedom, and so on. If we are able to see in this way, to approach the world and our lives with thankfulness, we make the world more what we hope for the world to be: a place worth being thankful for.

***

Josiah had never intentionally broken a law before, but here he was packing bologna sandwiches into baggies and stuffing apples and potato chips alongside them. He was going with some friends down to a city park to distribute food to anyone who showed up. They'd been doing this once a week for about a year now, but recently the city passed an ordinance prohibiting "organized food distribution" in city parks. The council said it was attracting the wrong kind of people and creating a disturbance.

Josiah looked at the hundreds of bagged meals he and his friends had prepared and he hoped that this expression of gratitude would create a big disturbance indeed.

Experiments in Thanks

■ The next time you eat out, after you've finished your meal, thank your server. Get up if you get a chance and thank your host—whoever it was who welcomed you into the restaurant. Ask to talk to the manager (this will make your server nervous, but reassure him or her), and tell the manager you enjoyed your meal, the service was great, and this place seems really well run. If you get a chance, thank the kitchen staff. After you get up and head for the door, sneak back and thank the person who clears the table into one of those big plastic bins. We guarantee you, you just made those people's day, because the service industry is thankless. Pay attention to how people respond to you, and how they react if you come back. (You might freak them out at first, so just be reassuring and gracious. They are freaked out because it is so rare that they are genuinely thanked.)

■ This Thanksgiving, or whenever there is a big, special meal in your culture, invite people who may not have anyone to share a meal with. There have got to be international students, or single parents without family nearby, or older people living alone near you. Go to work and make sure everyone has a place to go. The more different people you can invite, the better. When you're all eating together and getting to know each other, remember that this is God's table.

■ Sometime this year, maybe around the winter holidays, write out some thank-you cards for the people who make your everyday life possible, such as the person who delivers your heating oil, or the mail carrier, or the garbage collectors. Ideally, put a little money in the envelope—they love that. Give them these thank-you cards, and acknowledge what they do.

Love!

The eulogy was brief but powerful. "David was always known for his love of neighbors. When storms came, he helped rebuild. He was generous with his time, money, and energy. He brought his friends to church, and many are still members. He loved his neighbors, as Christ calls us to love, and he fought for them as well. In Vietnam, he fought our enemies overseas, and when he returned home, he fought to keep our borders secure as state senator, and then one of the Minutemen patrolling our borders. He did all he could to serve his neighbors, and he will be remembered for it. He loved just as Christ loved."

The Quintessential Christian Love

Most Christians, even those who aren't very loving, like to talk about love. "God is love," right? In a sense, very simple. Also tremendously vague. We use the same word to describe our feelings about our children, the McRib sandwich, Jesus, and the Chicago Blackhawks; the same word to refer to erotic feelings, romantic feelings, pride, trust, altruism, and patriotism. Love is a multifaceted word, and it can be stretched to accommodate any number of unloving feelings, thoughts, and actions.

The majority of love isn't all that special. Love is a very common, run-of-the-mill feeling, and the expression of that feeling is all over the place—in every religion and every culture. There isn't a culture that doesn't hold up love as a high ideal. Love is profoundly normal. Caught in a matrix of hormones, neurotransmitters, beliefs, traditions, behaviors, attraction, self-interest, and self-image lies love. Everybody does it. It is part of the basic package of human life.[1]

That God calls us to love ourselves is not at all extraordinary or radical. Any therapist or counselor or even a decent friend will tell us the same. It is easy to demonstrate the benefits of caring for oneself and of maintaining a strong and healthy self-image. It is clear that people who do not care for themselves fall apart emotionally and physically over time, hurting not just themselves but other people as well.

That God calls us to love our neighbors, and even strangers and "aliens" is nothing special. Loving our neighbors is very normal human behavior. We'll tend to approve of and support those people who are close to us, who look like us and act like us, without even thinking about it. Our neighbors may sometimes piss us off, but loving them isn't a stretch for most people. We can see the Bible witnessing to the expansion of this idea of neighbor-love to include strangers and travelers and indigent people, people who aren't literally neighbors but who are neighbor-like. This expansion of in-groups is necessary to civilization. If we were not capable of caring for people who were not part of our village or local tribe, there would be no large societies at all.

We can see this progression take a turn for the profoundly challenging, however, when we turn to the only quintessential Christian form of love. It isn't *agape*[2] (which, far from being quintessentially Christian, is borrowed from ancient Greek philosophy, and is even practiced in a limited form by chimps, bonobos, and Libertarians). The quintessential Christian form of love is the *love of enemies*. Ringing in our ears should be Jesus in his sermon proclaiming, "You have heard that it was said, 'You shall love your neighbor and hate

---

1. Here we are drawing on the work of, among many others, Doctors Richard Lewis Thomas, Amini Fari, and Richard Lannon, the authors of *A General Theory of Love* (New York: Random House, 2000).

2. Agape is one of four Greek words used for love. It means selfless love—as opposed to romantic love (eros), friendship (filia), and natural affection such as of a parent or a child (storge). When Dr. J.R. Daniel Kirk of Fuller Theological Seminary read a draft of this chapter he pointed out to us that the word agape is what the Septuagint uses to describe what Amnon feels for Tamar...before he rapes her (2 Samuel 13).

your enemy.' But I say to you, love your enemies."[3] Even when talking about neighbors in the story of the good Samaritan, Jesus expands "neighbor" to very clearly mean "enemy"—the Samaritan himself.[4] The call to love our enemies is inescapable for Christians, and there is no time in our history when we have not proven how terrible we are at it.

Unlike other kinds of love, enemy-love is not self-evident. Unlike every other form of love, we do not observe enemy-love in our primate relatives. We're not aware of any research or theory demonstrating how enemy-love would give a population an evolutionary advantage. No one falls into enemy-love the way they can fall into *eros, filia,* or even *agape.* Enemy-love stands apart from every other form of love because we see no society that broadly practices it—not in the present, nor in the historical record. You do not see it cross-culturally—quite the reverse. Every culture has its own methods for identifying and resisting or destroying enemies, and we can even generalize about this process and how it functions.

The apostle Paul famously said of love that it "always protects, always trusts, always hopes, always perseveres."[5] He was speaking at the time of loving that person in the church that you passionately dislike and never agree with, not about romantic love. The key characteristic of love in Paul's ode is its excessiveness. No student of moderation, love *always* protects, even when doing so means giving up its own life for the beloved. Love *always* trusts, even when it has been repeatedly betrayed. Love *always* hopes, even when it is obviously ridiculous to do so. Love *always* perseveres, even after death.

Love always does more than is required. Love is the "fulfillment of the law," as Jesus and some of his contemporaries put it, because it always goes beyond the law to give more than can be legally demanded.[6] Love of enemies is the pinnacle of love because it is the most surprising and the most difficult. Loving a friend means not keeping track of gifts and favors, and freely offering aid and comfort without expecting anything in return. Loving an enemy means responding to hatred with compassion, and answering violence

---

3. Matthew 5:43–48 (NRSV).
4. Luke 10:25–37.
5. 1 Corinthians 13:7 (NIV).
6. Matthew 22:34–40; Romans 13:8–10; Galatians 5:14.

with kindness. To love an enemy is to exceed justice and the law, to exceed even mercy, forbearance, and forgiveness.

If we are not loving our enemies, we are not being Christians—disciples and followers of Jesus Christ—whatever else we may be doing. We can remain cunningly disguised as Christians while we merely love our selves and families and neighbors and the occasional stranger, but the mark that sets disciples of Jesus Christ apart is the love of enemies.

Whatever You Forgive on Earth

ARIC

On Wednesday, September 21, 2011, two men were executed in the United States for racially tinged murders.

One was named Troy Davis, and his execution prompted protests around the world. Davis, a black man who always maintained his innocence, was convicted of the murder of Mark Macphail, a white off-duty police officer. No physical evidence ever emerged connecting Davis to the crime, and seven of the nine original witnesses later recanted, and some even claimed the police had coerced their testimony. All of Davis' appeals failed. No one granted him clemency, though many federal officials and celebrities, including the Pope, called for it. Millions held vigil while he was lethally injected and died. One family who did not protest his execution were the Macphails, who saw it as justice finally being served. "That's what we wanted, and that's what we got," they said.

The other man was named Lawrence Brewer. Along with two other men, Brewer was convicted of the murder of James Byrd Jr., who had his throat slit and was dragged behind a pickup truck until his head and limbs were severed from his body. Brewer never showed remorse for his crime. On the contrary, he was proud of it. While in prison he joined a white supremacist gang and wrote letters in which he boasted, "Well, I did it and no longer am I a virgin. It was a rush, and I'm still licking my lips for more." There were no mass protests of Brewer's execution. There were no celebrity calls for clemency. Indeed, it was hardly even mentioned in the media, except as a footnote on the Troy Davis story that another man was killed on the same night.

There was one family who held a vigil for Lawrence Brewer on the eve of his execution: the Byrds. "He has no remorse, and I feel sorry for him, but forgiveness brings about healing," Said Betty, daughter of James Byrd. Betty and her brother opposed the execution of their father's murderer, pleading with the state for a sentence of life imprisonment instead, but the gruesome crime had set political wheels in motion, which resulted in hate crime laws named after James Byrd Jr. being passed in Texas and at the federal level, which mandate harsher penalties for crimes motivated by hatred for specific minorities. The Byrds were demonstrating forgiveness in the face of a nation determined to mete out punishment. While the rest of us were finding better ways to protect ourselves from our enemies, the Byrds found a way to love their enemy instead.

Pseudo Enemy-Love

There is a kind of insincere graciousness amidst disagreement that is a form of spiritual violence. You have encountered this if you've ever had someone say, with a smile that doesn't quite reach their eyes, "I'm concerned for your salvation." Or perhaps you've been in a community where you were constantly told that you were welcome, but you were sent subtle signals implying that you would only be truly welcome once you changed. Maybe it was even worse and you or someone you know was kicked out of their home or expelled from their community, all the while being told it was done out of love to bring them to an awareness of their sin and the need for repentance. Perhaps you have noticed that people who parrot the aphorism "Love the sinner, hate the sin" are doing so to justify their hate, not their love.[7]

This kind of pseudo enemy-love is referred to in Proverbs, which is then quoted in Romans, in which we are told, "If your enemy is hungry, feed him; if he is thirsty, give him something to drink. In doing this, you will heap burning coals on his head."[8] Approached in this way, enemy-love becomes just another weapon, though one that is wielded passive-aggressively. With good cause, many people would prefer forthright aggression to sanctimonious condescension.

In defense of the writer of Proverbs and of the apostle Paul, we see a progression in scripture of increasingly more difficult forms of love. The kindness-as-cruelty form of love that the writer of Proverbs recommends is an intermediate step on the path to true enemy-love.

---

7. Professor and preacher Tony Campolo's pithy response to "Love the sinner, hate the sin" is, "That's just the opposite of what Jesus says Jesus never says, "love the sinner but hate his sin." Jesus says, "love the sinner and hate your own sin." http://youtu.be/gWYtkn_8D-g

8. Romans 12:20 (NIV); from Proverbs 25:21–22.

Biblical advice to be kind to your enemy as a way of shaming them is akin to the common wisdom, "If you can't say something nice, don't say anything at all," or that classic dismissive Southern phrase, "Bless your heart!" In essence, the writers of Proverbs are telling us, if we can't overcome the desire to hurt our enemies, then at least do it by conspicuous, humiliating generosity. If that's the best you can manage, it is better than an outright attack, but it is not in itself enough.

We are convinced that we can do better than this; indeed we think it is imperative. God is in the world reconciling all things.[9] Being fully reconciled to God means being fully reconciled with all that will be in and of God—including that person who despises you and has hurt you. God has claimed this person just as God has claimed you, and there will be no peace between you and God until there is peace between you and that person.

Psalm 23 contains the magnificent line, "You prepare a table before me in the presence of my enemies."[10] In various places in scripture God's intentions for creation are described in terms of a feast to which all of the nations of the world are invited.[11] Sitting at that table means sitting in the presence of your enemies. The kingdom of heaven is incomplete without your enemies there—or did you think that the only ones included would be the ones you like, the ones you agree with, the ones you find pleasing to be around?

Jesus ate with sinners and tax collectors—not reformed sinners and retired tax collectors, not ex-sinners and repentant tax collectors. Jesus did not say, "I will love you when you are good enough." Jesus didn't even say, "I will love you as long as you don't hurt me." Jesus loved all the way to the cross, loved from the cross, and loved after the cross as well.

That is why your enemies in your life right now are a gift from God. Whether they are co-workers, strangers, old friends, ex-lovers, or even your parents—the people who have hurt you and those you have hurt are your best hope of preparing for the kingdom. Without injuries to be forgiven, or wounds to beg pardon for, we could not get

---

9. 2 Corinthians 5:18–20; Colossians 1:15–20.

10. This is an atypical reading of the psalm and we're cool with that.

11. Isaiah 25:6–8; Zechariah 14:16; or in reference to the nations worshiping together on the mountain Zion: Psalm 65:2; Psalm 86:9; Isaiah 27:13, 49:7, 66:23; Revelation 15:4.

ready for the universal work of reconciliation that lies in the future. Thank God for your enemies, for they are the only ones who can teach you the most important form of love.

Love the Enemy Within

The possibility of true enemy-love starts very close to home. It starts with loving the enemy inside your own skin. No one in your entire life will hurt you, will sabotage your goals and undermine your best efforts to change, will say cruel and callous things about you and tear you down as much as...you. For many of us the most difficult aspect of Jesus' commandment that we love our neighbors as ourselves is learning not to despise ourselves in the first place. Tragically, self-loathing can even masquerade as humility, and many false martyrs have been applauded for their noble sacrifices, which were in truth acts of self-harm.[12]

To some Christians the advice to love yourself sounds like the sort of thing a life coach might say, but hardly Christlike. Others, nurtured on a steady diet of pop-psychology and finding-yourself storylines are ready to put this book down right now and go take a spa day. But we are not referring to either narcissism on the one hand, or self-esteem on the other. We don't want you to discover your inner beauty. To quote *Fight Club*, "You are not a beautiful and unique snowflake."[13]

Loving the enemy that lives inside you begins with being awake enough to see clearly. It means really looking in a mirror and perceiving what is there without embellishment, either to protect your ego or to abuse the stranger looking back at you. Vision that precise usually requires good friends who aren't afraid to be that mirror for you.[14] Once you see yourself clearly, you will see your flaws, your weakness, the ways in which you are still enslaved. You will recognize your enemy. This is the person you are to find a way to love.

There is a ridiculous and unfortunate misunderstanding, seemingly common among Christians, that it is necessary to neglect oneself in order to truly love and serve others. This Christian falsehood

---

12. Consider the example of Clare of Assisi suffering from Anorexia Nervosa in our chapter "Beg!"

13. "You are not a beautiful and unique snowflake. You are the same decaying organic matter as everyone else, and we are all part of the same compost pile." Tyler Durden in *Fight Club*, by Chuck Palahniuk (New York: W. W. Norton and Company, 1996).

14. Consider our discussion of Wasting Each Other's Time in "Confess!"

has a parallel in the ridiculous and unfortunate misunderstanding that pervades all of Western culture and economics—that we can only benefit at a cost to others. Both of these are ways we fail to understand love.

Entwined in this concept of loving the enemies within and around us is the matter of self-protection. It is crucial to understand that we are not telling those in abusive relationships to stay there out of a desire to "love" their abuser into change or reconciliation. Abusive relationships are destructive to all parties involved. In these circumstances the most loving act that can be taken is to leave. Remaining in an abusive relationship is *not* enemy-love; it is self-hatred. To love both the enemy within ourselves and the enemy embodied by our abuser, we must break the cycle.[15]

Loving ourselves as we love others are not two separate challenges—they are the same. If you do not love yourself well, you cannot possibly love others well. If you cannot face the person in the mirror with grace and understanding, you cannot honestly face anyone else. Similarly, no matter how much you pamper and reward the person in the mirror, if you do this by depriving others, even many steps removed, you are not practicing love, but rather a sad, pedestrian form of self-worshiping idolatry.

Love your neighbors as you love yourself: you will love your neighbors only insofar as you love yourself, and you cannot love yourself without loving others. Love your neighbors as you love yourself: when you come to understand that love of self is connected inextricably to love of others, you will be better at doing both.

"A Wizard of Earthsea" (Spoiler Alert)

DOUG

One of my all-time favorite books is A Wizard of Earthsea *by Ursula K. LeGuin. It is like an older and more literary Harry Potter—the kind of Harry Potter you'd imagine LeGuin having written: all about moral choices and characters gaining wisdom, in the context of a story of a gifted boy going to a magical school.*

The main character is named Ged. As a child and then as an adolescent, Ged shows a natural ability with magic, which in Earthsea

---

15. For further theological exploration, check out *Proverbs of Ashes: Violence, Redemptive Suffering, and the Search for What Saves Us* by Rita Nakashima Brock and Rebecca Ann Parker (Boston: Beacon Press, 2001).

is a matter of knowing the true natures and names of the things around you. Early on, Ged falls under the tutelage of an older wizard named Ogion. Ogion tries to teach him patience and wisdom, but Ged is flush with his talent and power, and Ogion decides that he may do better at the School on Roke Island.

Ged runs afoul of another student, and they become rivals. Flush with his own power and wanting to show up his rival, Ged says that he will summon the spirit of a dead person. He overreaches, however, and during the ritual, a terrible shadow escapes. It attacks Ged, cutting his face with its claws, and nearly kills him. Healing him takes all of the strength of the Archmage of Roke, who subsequently dies. Ged, thoroughly chastised, finally finishes his schooling, but his talent and power seem to have gone, and he is no more than an ordinary student. He takes a position serving a small collection of boring islands as their local wizard.

As time goes on, it becomes clear to Ged that he has to deal with this Shadow that he has loosed upon the world. It continues to hunt and haunt him, and to threaten those near him. He flees the Shadow for a long time, but comes to a point where he can flee it no more. He turns to hunting it down, and finds that the Shadow flees him when he does so.

As I said, the magic of Earthsea is rooted in knowing the true names of persons, places, and things. Ged must face this Shadow, but he doesn't know it's true name—it's a monster from the realm of the dead; maybe it has no name. At the final confrontation, however, LeGuin delivers one of the main messages of the book. Ged finally finds the Shadow, meets it at the edge of the known world, and calls it by its true name—which is, of course, Ged. The Shadow was set loose by his arrogance—it is his Shadow, and no other. Ged and the Shadow embrace, leaving only a much wiser Ged behind.

I think we are like that, and that is what LeGuin is trying to illustrate through this story. We seek to divide ourselves: trying to keep the good parts we like, while ignoring the bad parts we don't like. Meanwhile, people around us are hurt, and we never heal, never come to terms with the things we do, never take responsibility. If we can't even name who we really are, how can we ever hope to love?

Love the Enemy at the Gates

The love of enemies defines Christian political engagement. This is not to say that enemy-love defines the political engagement of most Christians out there. For most Christians, political engagement occurs in accordance with political rules—choose a side, and hammer on the other side until you have enough leverage to win and impose your will. This is the logic of advocacy and voting, of lobbying and protest. It is the logic of warfare, but in political engagement the weapons are words and ideas and public action.

For most Christians, political engagement focuses on homosexuality, abortion, and, occasionally, when the mood strikes, something such as ecology or, on the very fringe, issues of war and economic injustice. But if someone mentions that a public figure is a committed Christian, how many would then think, "Oh, he must love his enemies!"

When Christians do not love their political enemies, they are not being Christians, they are just misappropriating the term. Enemy-love is genuine love of the person, in the midst of disagreements and conflict over deeply held values—love of the person even as that person espouses things that you genuinely hate. This is not loving people because they are attractive, or convincing, or virtuous, or even tolerable for the most part. This is loving them because God loves them.

Enemy-love is not reducible to a political strategy, such as nonviolent direct action. Nonviolent direct action may be carried out with or without love, with or without care and concern for the people one is acting directly against. Enemy-love is not doing nothing, not passivity in the face of evil and injustice. It is not pretending there are not differences—pretending there is no right and wrong, no good and no evil.

When Jesus talks about loving our enemies, he uses concrete, even measurable, examples. Jesus makes loving your enemy into something like a S.M.A.R.T. goal.[16] When faced with a political and religious enemy who is lying on the side of the road, beaten, you pick him up, even though it makes you unclean and brings your errand to a halt, and you bring him to a place where he can be cared for, and you pay for his care, and come check up on him later to make sure all is well. If you are forced at sword point to carry a centurion's gear for a mile, carry it for a second mile. See if you can make it so the centurion has to ask for his own pack back. If someone strikes you on the face

---

16. This is a goal that is Simple (or Specific), Measurable, Attainable, Relevant, and Time-bound—a common acronym in leadership and business training circles.

dismissively, the way someone would hit a slave, make it so they have to strike you as an equal if they hit you a second time. If someone takes your coat because you owe them money, give them the rest of your clothes as well, as a way to call attention to the inequity of the situation.[17]

None of these acts are feeble—all of them require great courage. They are love given flesh. It is not enough to pretend that you feel love for your enemies. You must behave as if you love them, even when they hurt you and themselves. Keep your dignity while you do this— love yourself in the midst of it—but love them as well. Love them not in a way that makes them feel warm and fuzzy at the expense of what is right, nor in a way that protects your social standing in an unjust status quo. Love them in a way that gives life, and restores dignity, and opens a door for repentance, if needed, and reconciliation.

Devastating Our Own

NICK

Failing to love our enemies is not only bad for them, it's also devastating for us—leaving us morally injured. Moral injury is a type of psychological trauma; it's a deep-seated sense of moral transgression that includes feelings of shame, meaninglessness, and remorse from having violated one's core moral beliefs. When we send men and women into the horror of war, they must violate the core moral values of civilized society. More simply stated, when we fail to love our enemies, something inside us breaks.

I was first introduced to this concept by Rita Nakashima Brock.[18] This incredibly intelligent pacifist, feminist theologian was the last person I would expect to be working with soldiers, but in doing so she taught me a great deal about enemy-love—not because Rita is enemies with our soldiers, but because she spoke adamantly about the harm we inflict on our soldiers by asking them to commit violent acts that are against their moral selves.

Enemy-love refuses to make soldiers decide whether or not they should engage a child soldier, or put them in a situation in which they have to make a split-second decision as to whether someone is reaching for a cell

---

17. Matthew 5:38–42. It is possible to do this in such a way as to shame one's enemy, but we read this passage similarly to how Martin Luther King Jr. and Walter Wink read it: that the goal is to restore right relationship rather than to coerce.

18. Rita Nakashima Brock, *Soul Repair: Recovering from Moral Injury after War* (Boston: Beacon Press, 2012) has an excellent in-depth look at this subject.

phone or a gun. When they have to make those decisions, right or wrong, they are left broken inside. When we hurt others, we injure our own souls too. It is necessary to love our enemies for our own sake, as well as for theirs.

Our Enemy, Who Art in Heaven

It is one thing to imagine loving enemies who hurt us in our lives—people like us, with all the limitations and difficulties that are part of the human condition—but what about the divine condition? What about when God is the enemy?

How is it that God could be our enemy? God is the enemy when we have begged day and night to be relieved of a mental illness or addiction, and in despair finally give up hope of ever changing. God is the enemy when we stand in the emergency room looking down at the broken body of a loved one. God is the enemy when parents bury their children. God is the enemy when a parent tries to change his or her child's sexual orientation with abuse dressed up as "therapy," or, if that doesn't work, beat it out of that child. God is the enemy when clergy protect each other instead of victims of their abuse. God is the enemy when children are coerced into "accepting Jesus as their personal Savior" before they are old enough to drive, much less vote.

There are times when, as far as we can tell, God fails us; when Abba is a deadbeat, absentee father in our lives; when we cry to the heavens and are answered with an echoing silence. With the Psalms and Lamentations, we cry out to God, "When will you remember your people?" With Job we rage, "Answer me, God!" With Jesus dying in agony on the cross, we sob, "My God, my God, why have you forsaken me?" We beg, we wheedle, we barter, we cajole, and the fact is that sometimes God is not there, and in most of the troubles in our lives, if not all of them, God will not intervene in a way we can identify with any certainty.

We are left alone, in the darkness, betrayed by God. In this moment, what we truly believe is tested. Do we love our enemies merely because we can lean on God like a crutch? Do we depend on God to be the one who really loves our enemies because we just can't? Or have we learned to follow in Jesus' path, and love even the enemy God who abandons us at our moments of greatest need?

The quintessential Christian love is the love of enemies, and this includes when God is our enemy. In scripture, generations pass during which it seems that God has abandoned God's own people—generations of slavery in Egypt, generations of warfare and exploitation and defeat at the hands of the Babylonians, generations of exiles weeping by the waters of the Euphrates, generations of repressive Roman rule and the failed Maccabean revolts, generations of early Christians tortured to death because they would confess only one Lord, and it was not Caesar. This suffering was real, and the experience of abandonment by God is real. It is not enough to merely say, "It all works out for the best in the end," because this is often not apparent, if it is ever true. Most of the time, when we suffer, we don't know why, and we are wise not to trust those who offer easy, formulaic answers.

To love God when God is our enemy is to continue in relationship with God even when this relationship seems one-sided. To love God the enemy is to trust the things that we have learned in our lives through our relationship with God—about ourselves, about others, about what it means to be Christlike in a Christ-killing world. To love God the enemy is to trust those who are with us on this journey—that they will care for us even when God does not. To love God the enemy is to leave our doors open to await God's return, like a father seeing our prodigal son coming down the road toward us. We welcome God's return because we love our enemy.[19]

Jesus Is the Enemy

There is no enemy who is not also Jesus to us; there is no enemy whom Jesus does not already love. There is no one, nothing, outside the reach of Christ's love, and therefore there should be no one, nothing, outside the reach of Christian love. Sometimes, when we conclude worship and are ready to go back out into the world, we say something like this as a benediction, a good word: "Love God with all your heart, your soul, your mind, and your strength; and love your neighbors as yourselves." From Christ and the early church we see that this love means the love of enemies, not just loving people who are easy to love.

---

19. Luke 15:11–32. This reading of the famous parable was suggested to us in "Parable of the Prodigal Father," from Peter Rollins, *The Orthodox Heretic and Other Impossible Tales* (Brewster, Mass.: Paraclete Press, 2009).

Christian love is the love of ourselves: specifically the darkness inside of us, the propensity to do harm and to fail to do good, and the delight we take in our wrongdoing. Christian love is the love of our neighbors: not just the kind, neighborly ones, but the bastards and the assholes and the nasty, petty, hurtful people in our lives. This love does not sugarcoat who they are or what they do, but rather finds Christ in them and reacts to that God-image rather than the way it has become corrupted. Christian love is love of God with everything we have, and when God is our enemy, when God is silent and distant, it takes all we have to continue loving.

We love our enemies because we find Christ in them. The violence we pour out on our enemies, we pour upon Christ. When we love our enemies, we also love Christ. It may even be that, in some moment of in-breaking possibility, our enemies find that our love illuminates Christ inside of them. Love awakens love; mercy inspires mercy; healing calls out to those who are broken. It may be that when we love our enemies, seeing the image of God in them, that they see the image of God in themselves, and are changed, even redeemed.

Whether they change or not, however, we love them.

***

Everyone had told Moira not to do it. This gave the memorial service a strange air of judgment. Mixed with the expressions of grief were glances that said, "I told you so." Even the ones who had supported her couldn't help but think she'd brought this on herself to a degree. She went as a civilian to the warzone. She lived among the enemy, helping supply clinics with bandages and medicine and putting her statistical skills to work keeping an unofficial casualty count updated online. She was sitting in a cafe to use their wi-fi when she became a casualty herself in an errant drone strike. When Moira's mother stood up to give the eulogy, she ignored the disapproving eyes and simply asked, "Who has the courage to continue her work?"

Experiments in Love

■ Commit to gradual disarmament. If you own literal weapons, only keep the ones that you think Jesus Christ would use on someone. For the rest, give them to one of those buy-back programs, or turn them over to the police. Think about the weapons you use socially—dismissive charm, derisive humor, or glowering until people figure out what you want. Give up one thing at a time. Go as slow as you want, but keep going. Every time you disarm, reward yourself, and think about how you are more like Jesus.

■ Break bread with your enemy. Choose neutral ground and meet up with them and share a meal. Go Dutch so that nobody gets testy about who will pay. Make awkward small talk, or reconcile, or confront them about their behavior—but, whatever you do, be harmless and only act or speak when it is in the best interest of both of you.

■ Forgive God—for every question not answered, for every unjust thing you have suffered, for every crappy or painful thing you never asked for and didn't deserve. Even if you no longer believe in God, or never did, imagine you are talking to God, and this is how you are saying goodbye. If you do believe in God, take this opportunity to start out on a new footing.

Go and Do!

There are an infinite variety of ways to create a picture of the Christian life. You might start like a painter with a blank canvas, layering on colors and framing shapes until an image emerges. You might treat it like a mosaic, placing tiny piece after tiny piece in precise order until the whole coalesces. In this book, we have approached the task more like a sculptor chiseling away mass, seeking to reveal what lies beneath.

Sometimes words and ideas get used so much for so long, and accumulate such baggage, that they become unwieldy. They lose their vitality and choke out the very purpose for which they were coined. It does no good to attempt to layer on new meaning. This just adds to the detritus. You have to start chiseling—removing meaning, sweeping away assumptions, casting out sacred cows—to get to something you can grasp.

We named this book *Never Pray Again* because it is our conviction that prayer is one of these ideas that has too much baggage to do its job anymore. In our own lives, it needed to be set free from the rock imprisoning it before it could be much use. We noticed as we looked at the ancient liturgical structure of worship, and examined each type of prayer usually found there, that if we simply removed the word "prayer" we unleashed something vital and compelling. Instead of prayers of praise, you just have the imperative: "Praise!" Instead of praying your confession, you are urged to "Confess!" Instead of pleading privately for help from God, you're compelled to publicly "Beg!"

In this book we have sought to seize something immediate, direct, and surprising. *Immediate*: meaning that it is not something attainable only through esoteric knowledge, or practice, or extreme commitment. *Direct*: meaning that it applies interpersonally here and now, and not only in some spiritual or abstract sense. *Surprising*: meaning that we tried to ask what might lie behind and beyond the popular understanding of these ideas.

Through these pages we've tried to not only whittle away conceptual baggage layered on spiritual practice; we've also tried to remove obstacles that get in the way of holy living. Prayer itself serves too easily as that thing we do instead of acting more directly and more powerfully. We have not tried to write a list of things to do, but rather to remove all the excuses we have for not doing what we already know we must. We encourage you to carve out less time for prayer and less time for spiritual practices that steal time away from going and doing.

The world urgently needs people who are awake, who know how to expel demons, and who aren't afraid to intercede for others. We have spent far too much time on bended knee teaching ourselves to whisper words to a transcendent God and pretending that love is a feeling inside us rather than something we must do in the world. It is time we lifted our heads, unclasped our hands, and got to work. Whether we ever pray again or not, who we are has more to do with how we treat each other than what we say in our heart.

Nothing stands between you and abundant life. All that remains is for you to go and do.